The Cake
Cook Book

LILITH RUSHING

RUTH VOSS

The Cake

Cook Book

CHILTON BOOKS—Publishers

A Division of Chilton Company

Philadelphia and New York

℘ Acknowledgments

We wish to thank the following for their help and encouragement in the preparation of this book:

Our sisters: Sybil Hancock, Coral Sanford, Vera Brannon and Ethel Brannon, for helping us to test the recipes and for letting us use their own favorite recipes.

Joanne Snider, the daughter of Ruth Voss; Emma Stephenson, her niece; Sue Breeden, Hilda Bracey and Fay Cantrell, nieces of Lilith Rushing. They also tested many recipes for us and gave some to us.

Our friend, Mrs. Alberta Bennight, who kindly gave us her mother's recipe, *Mrs. Alice Peet's Eggless Cake*.

The many other relatives and friends who have throughout the years given us their treasured recipes.

The J. C. Ferguson Publishing Company of Chicago, who allowed us to include the *Cocoa Coconut Cake, Half-A-Pound Cake* and *Whole Wheat Cake* from the "Modern Family Cook Book" by Meta Given, copyright 1953.

The Wichita Eagle and Beacon, who granted permission for the inclusion from their *Home Town News* by Frank Good, copyright 1961, of *Wacky Cake, Crazy Cake, Angel Delight Cake, Rhubarb Upside Down Cake* and *Green Apple Cake*.

Chilton Books for letting us include *Common Causes and Remedies in Cake Baking Failures* from "The Gold Cook Book" by Louis P. DeGouy, copyright 1947, 1948.

And last, but very far from least, Luther Rushing, husband of Lilith Rushing, cake-lover extraordinary, who has over the years courted dyspepsia by tasting every baked product that emanated from his wife's oven and continues to ask for more.

In compiling this book we made no attempt to include the many cakes that are native to various foreign countries, but chose to confine ourselves to those that can truly be said are home-made in America.

LILITH RUSHING
RUTH VOSS

WICHITA, KANSAS
March 1965

℞ Contents

viii   *CONTENTS*

A fair lady once said, "Let them eat cake!"
  the history books record, there on the shelf,
We repeat, "Let them eat cake!"
  and homemaker dear, make it yourself!

Before
You Begin

HOW TO USE THIS BOOK

All measurements given are level, unless otherwise stated. We recommend the use of standard metal measuring cups with level tops and a set of standard measuring spoons.

"Butter" can be butter or margarine. However, natural butter gives the richest flavor and finest texture to cake and, if possible, its use is recommended. If country or dairy butter is a definite requirement, the fact is so stated in the recipe. The other recipes are adapted for the specific type of shortening listed. However, butter may be substituted in the following proportions:

1 cup butter equals ⅞ cup of solid or liquid oil or shortening (½ cup butter equals 8 tablespoons)

Thus, in replacing shortening with butter, use about one-eighth additional butter.

Sift all flour and confectioners sugar before measuring. If granulated sugar has "packed" in its box, that too should be sifted before measuring.

All the recipes in this book call for the use of standard SAS Double Action baking powder.

Fill baking pans about half full, but never more than two-thirds full, although loaf and tube pans may be filled a little higher.

Abbreviations Used

Tbsp. = tablespoon
tsp. = teaspoon
doz. = dozen
pkg. = package
lb. = pound
oz. = ounce

We have tried to catalogue these recipes so that the home baker can easily find the cake she wants to make. But many a kind overlaps another. Please consult the Index at back of the book which is cross-referenced.

All the cakes in this book have been tested and used over and over by homemakers.

3

THE INGREDIENTS OF A CAKE

The principal cake ingredients are flour, sugar, shortening, eggs, milk (or other liquid), baking powder (or other leavening), flavoring, and salt. Each has its own effect upon the success of the cake.

Flour

The flour absorbs and holds considerable moisture and aids in holding the other ingredients together. It also assists materially in building up and maintaining the skeletal structure of the cake.

There are various types of flour, each of which is preferable for a specific class of cakes. For instance, pound cake, fruit cake and cakes of the "heavier" type require a cake flour of higher gluten-protein content than do layer cakes, whereas angel food and sponge cakes need a cake flour of lower and softer gluten content.

The principal kinds of flour are bread flour, all-purpose, and cake flour. And although flour accounts for only a small percentage of the total cost of the cake, the wrong type of flour or an inferior grade can easily ruin the finished product. Therefore it is false economy for the cake baker to use anything but high quality flour of a type best suited for the specific recipe she is making.

Sugar

Sugar is a most important ingredient in cakes and should be used in exactly the correct proportions and should be carefully incorporated into the cake. As a whole, sugar serves the following important purposes in cake making: it adds sweetness; it aids in the creaming process; it creates a softening or spreading action in the batter; it imparts color to the crust; it retains moisture, thereby prolonging the cake's freshness; it forms the body of icings and fillings; it adds food value.

Excessive amounts of sugar tend to cause a thick, porous crust, coarse grain, and a soggy texture. They may make a cake rise well at first, but it will fall while baking. Insufficient sugar often means a low volume cake with a tough, coarse interior, and with inferior keeping qualities.

Sugar is usually creamed in with the shortening and eggs prior to addition of the other ingredients. In some cakes, part of the sugar is added with the flour.

Shortening

With the exception of angel food and some types of sponge cake, in which no shortening is used, the judicious use of shortening in nearly all cakes aids materially in the creation of the desired volume, grain and texture. The shortening, which is uniformly distributed throughout the mixed mass of cake ingredients, coats each tiny particle of batter, giving to the crumb of the finished product a long lasting softness. This means that the cake will retain its freshness for a longer period.

Butter, margarine, vegetable shortenings, liquid oils (corn and vegetable), and cream, are the principal shortening agents used in cakes. Each type has its purpose and the cake baker should follow recipe directions in the use of shortening.

Eggs

The primary function of eggs in cake is their effect on the eating qualities of the cake.

If whole eggs or yolks are used the cake has a pleasing golden color, giving it a definite appetite appeal. In such cakes as angel food, where only the egg whites are used, the snowy whiteness that results from the prolonged beating or whipping is especially desirable.

The beating of eggs forms a fluffy, foam-like mass which is much lighter and occupies a much larger volume than do unbeaten eggs. Thus, the air is incorporated and distributed throughout the cake batter and, when subjected to the heat of the oven, the expansion of this air exerts a definite leavening action on the cake.

In conjunction with the gluten of flour, eggs act as the supporting framework of a cake and therefore have a marked influence on the grain and texture of the cake. Eggs also impart a delicious flavor to the cake, and the nutritive value of eggs needs no explanation.

Milk

Milk helps to prolong the freshness of the cake, assists in promoting a desirable appearance, and helps to prevent greasiness. Milk also adds to the richness and flavor of the cake as well as to its food value.

Whole sweet milk, buttermilk or sour milk, dried milk, condensed and evaporated milk are used in different types of cakes. The kind called for in each recipe is planned to harmonize with the other ingredients.

Baking Powder

Baking powder is the principal leavening agent of cakes. While other ingredients can be considered the "body" of a cake, it is the action of baking powder that is mainly responsible for the conversion of the heavy mass of batter into a light, well-risen, appetizing cake. Thus, baking powder may be called the "soul" of a cake.

It is very important to use the exact amount of baking powder. Lack of volume, poor grain and texture, and impaired eating qualities are likely to result if either too little or too much baking powder is used. However, it is better to use too little than too much.

Since even the most carefully preserved baking powder can, and frequently does, deteriorate and lose its leavening action, it is suggested that a newly opened can, or one which has stood on the shelf for a time, be tested before using. To do this mix a teaspoon of the powder in one-third cup of hot water. If the powder bubbles vigorously it is in good condition; should it fail to bubble or do so only feebly, do not use it.

Flavoring

The proper use of flavoring can greatly enhance a cake, and the careless or improper use of flavoring can just as readily ruin the quality of what would otherwise have been a good cake.

Cake is made up largely of rich ingredients which in proper proportions and blended together in the cake create a naturally delicious flavor. This is further improved by the judicious use of flavoring.

Lemon and vanilla extract are the most commonly used flavorings, with vanilla probably the most popular. Vanilla blends exceptionally well with the shortening in cake, particularly with butter. Other popular flavorings are chocolate, cocoa, spices, brown sugar and molasses, almond extract, ginger, and orange.

In order to please the palate, the final flavor of the cake must represent a harmony of the individual flavors of which it is composed. The flavor should not be too strong but rather mildly tantalizing. If a predominant flavor is desired, it is often better to emphasize this flavor in the icing rather than in the cake itself. Harmonious flavorings make a taste-pleasing cake.

There are on the market many synthetic flavorings. It is heartily recommended that only pure extracts be used, for only these give the true essence of the desired flavor to the cake.

Salt

The main purpose of salt in cakes is its peculiar ability to bring out and intensify the inherent flavors of the cake and its ingredients. Without salt a cake would not *fall* flat but it would *taste* flat.

BASIC TOOLS FOR CAKE MAKING

1 set of mixing bowls of assorted sizes
2 nests of level measuring cups (1 for liquids; 1 for dry ingredients)
1 set of standard measuring spoons
3 spatulas of different sizes
1 rubber spatula
1 large slotted spoon (for separating eggs)
1 large wooden mixing spoon
1 rotary egg beater
1 long wire whisk (for beating egg whites)
1 short wire whisk (for whipping and general beating)
1 nut or spice grater
1 large flour sieve
1 large strainer
1 small strainer
1 lemon squeezer
1 paring knife
1 apple corer
1 wire cake rack (two-layer size)
1 wooden board (for chopping and for crushing crumbs)
1 oven thermometer
1 timer
1 10-inch cast iron skillet
1 2-quart double boiler
3 7-inch round layer cake pans

3 8-inch round layer cake pans
2 9-inch round layer cake pans
1 8-inch square baking pan
1 9-inch square baking pan
1 9-inch spring form pan
1 9-inch tube cake pan
1 10-inch tube cake pan
6 oblong loaf cake pans in assorted sizes from 7 to 15 inches
2 muffin tins
1 8-inch pie tin
1 9-inch pie tin
1 $15\frac{1}{2} \times 10\frac{1}{2} \times \frac{1}{2}$-inch jelly roll pan
1 large roll wax paper
1 large roll aluminum foil
1 box of wooden toothpicks (for testing)

"HOW TO"—A GLOSSARY OF BAKING TERMS AND PROCEDURES

Adding Flour and Liquid Alternately

This is important in order to keep the consistency of the batter as uniform as possible.

First, about one-fourth of the flour should be sifted and stirred in gently round and round with a wooden mixing spoon. Then the mixture should be beaten with a wire whisk until it is smooth. Next, about one-third of the liquid should be introduced in the same way. This procedure is then continued until all the flour and the liquid have been incorporated. Begin and end this process with an insertion of flour.

Adding Beaten Egg Whites

Use the "cut and fold" method. (See below.)

Beat the whites in a mixing bowl until they "peak" stiff and dry (stand up in sharp points) or "peak" stiff but not dry (stand up in softly rounded mounds) as called for in recipes. Use a long wire whisk.

Adding Beaten Whole Eggs

Beat the eggs with a rotary egg beater or short wire whisk until they are thick and light. Halfway beating only liquifies the eggs. So be sure the eggs are either unbeaten or *well* beaten.

Adding Whole Eggs (Unbeaten)

Drop the eggs, one at a time, right into the creamed sugar-shortening mixture and then beat *vigorously* with the wire whisk. Spirited beating is especially important when eggs are added unbeaten. The mixture should be lifted up while beating to enclose as much air as possible. Beating should be continued until each egg is thoroughly blended, then long enough thereafter to produce a light and smooth mixture.

To Beat (Use a Mixing Spoon or Wire Whisk)

Beating is a different motion from stirring. To beat, rapidly lift up the batter from the bottom of the bowl over and over. This blends the ingredients and introduces air into the mixture.

To Blanch Almonds (Remove Their Skins)

Cover the shelled nuts with boiling water, simmer for 1 minute on top of the stove, and then drain off the water. Rinse the almonds in cold water. Press the nuts between thumb and first and second fingers—the skins will slip off easily.

To Blend

This simply means to stir two or more ingredients together thoroughly.

To Brush

To spread a substance thinly over a surface with a small soft brush or with a piece of paper or cloth.

To Chill

To allow a mixture to become completely cold but not to freeze.

To Cream

The shortening or the sugar, or a mixture of both, is worked against the sides and bottom of a mixing bowl with the back of a spatula or wooden spoon until the mixture is smooth and plastic.

The shortening should be creamed separately first, then about 2 Tbsp. of sugar should be added and creaming continued. The remaining sugar is added in 3 or 4 portions with thorough creaming after each addition.

When all the sugar has been put in, the creaming is continued until the mixture is fluffy, light and creamy (not grainy or crumbly).

To Crumble

To break into small pieces with the fingers.

To Cut and Fold In

A rhythmic cutting down, lifting up, and folding over motion with a rubber spatula or wooden spoon. This motion keeps all the air bubbles in the feathery batter of angel and chiffon cakes. It should be done quickly, but carefully and thoroughly, until all the dry ingredients have disappeared.

To Cut In

Using two knives, to distribute a solid shortening throughout flour or other dry ingredients.

To Dot

To scatter small bits of something over a surface.

To Dust

To sprinkle lightly (usually flour or powdered sugar) over a surface.

To Flour

To cover with a light film of flour.

To Grease and Flour a Pan

Dip a piece of paper or cloth in shortening and spread evenly over the inside of a pan (the bottom more generously, the sides very lightly). Then dust some flour over it, shake the pan to spread the flour around, turn the pan upside down and knock out any excess flour.

To Knead

To stretch dough with the hands, folding it over and then pressing down on it with the heels of the palms. (Spread a large piece of wax paper on the table, or a clean dish towel, dust it very lightly with flour and stretch the dough on it.)

To Melt Chocolate

Do *not* do this over direct heat. Place the chocolate in the top of a double boiler over boiling water. Or place the chocolate in a small bowl that will fit into the top of a boiling tea kettle.

To Preheat

Set the oven to the required temperature and allow at least 10 to 15 minutes for it to warm up. If the oven has no caloric heat regulator, use an oven thermometer to indicate when the needed temperature has been reached, then lower the flame to maintain an even temperature and watch the thermometer while the cake is baking so as to raise or lower the oven flame if need be.

To Remove Cake from Pan

All cakes should be left in their baking pans for 3 to 5 minutes after removal from the oven. Then a knife or spatula should be run gently down between the side of the pan and the cake and run all around, easing lightly but firmly at corners of the pan. After that the pan can be turned over and a gentle shake will loosen the cake onto a plate or rack. Butter cakes should be left on a wire rack until they are completely cool.

An angel cake or sponge cake should be turned upside down in its pan as soon as it is removed from the oven. It should stand this way (supported by the tube of the pan) for about 1 hour. It may then be removed from the pan.

To Scald

To heat to just below the boiling point.

To Separate Egg Yolks from Whites

The old standby is to crack the egg as near its middle as possible so the egg will break approximately in half. Hold the yolk in one half and let the whites fall into a bowl. The yolk can be passed from one half eggshell to the other until all the white is extracted. Then the yolk can be dropped into a cup or another bowl.

The yolk can also be separated by using a large slotted spoon. Place the spoon over a cup or bowl, break the egg into it, and the whites will run through the slots.

A third method is to puncture a small hole in one end of the egg and let the whites flow out into a bowl. (The yolk can be kept in the shell for several days if the hole is sealed with tape and the egg returned to the refrigerator.)

To Sift

To pass through a sieve.

To Simmer

To cook in liquid on top of a stove at just below boiling point.

To Sliver Almonds

With a sharp knife, cut each nut into several pieces, from the pointed end to the base. Spread the pieces on a baking sheet or pie tin and dry them in a 350° oven for 10 minutes. (Slivering should be done while almonds are still warm from blanching.)

"Spins a Thread"

This means that a syrup falls from a spoon in a threadlike stream about 3 to 4 inches long, rather than falling in droplets.

To Whip

To beat rapidly and continuously with a wire whisk, a rotary beater, or with a fork.

MEASUREMENTS AND EQUIVALENTS

1 pint	equals	2 cups
1 cup	"	16 Tbsp. or 8 fluid oz.
¾ cup	"	12 Tbsp. or 6 fluid oz.
⅔ cup	"	10 Tbsp. plus 2 tsp.
½ cup	"	8 Tbsp. or 4 fluid oz.
⅓ cup	"	5 Tbsp. plus 1 tsp.
¼ cup	"	4 Tbsp. or 2 fluid oz.
⅛ cup	"	2 Tbsp. or 1 fluid oz.
1 Tbsp.	"	3 tsp. or ½ fluid oz.

1 lb. all-purpose flour, sifted	equals	4 cups
1 lb. all-purpose flour, unsifted	"	3½ cups
1 lb. cake flour, sifted	"	4½ cups
1 lb. cake flour, unsifted	"	4 cups
1 lb. confectioners sugar, sifted	"	4 cups
1 lb. granulated sugar	"	2 cups
1 lb. brown sugar	"	2½ cups, firmly packed
1 lb. shortening (any kind)	"	2 cups
¼ lb. butter	"	1 stick, or ½ cup, or 8 Tbsp.
1 lb. chopped walnuts	"	4 cups
1 cup egg whites	"	whites of 8–10 eggs
1 cup egg yolks	"	yolks of 12–14 eggs
1 cup fresh whole eggs	"	5–6 eggs
1 oz. baking powder	"	2⅔ Tbsp.
1 oz. baking soda	"	2 Tbsp.
1 oz. cream of tartar	"	3 Tbsp.
1 cup lemon juice	"	4–6 lemons

℞ General Instructions

1) Set out and check all needed ingredients, pans, bowls, tools, etc. before you start to mix.

2) Allow shortening and eggs to stand at room temperature for at least a half hour before they are used.

3) Preheat the oven to the indicated temperature before the cake is inserted.

4) Before creaming shortening, pour boiling water into the mixing bowl to heat it. Drain and dry the bowl thoroughly. If shortening is placed in a warm bowl it will cream more readily.

5) Measure all ingredients accurately, as follows:

Liquids Use only standard level-topped measuring cups, but if a lipped measuring cup should be used, check the mark by lifting the cup to eye level.

Solid Shortening (*If Measured Sticks of Butter or Margarine Are Not Used*) Use metal measuring cups and fill them firmly with a rubber spatula. Level off the excess with the straight edge of a spatula or knife.

Flour Sift through a sieve. Then spoon into a measuring cup until it overflows. Remove the excess lightly with a straight-edge knife or a spatula. (Do not press down the flour or shake the cup to level it.)

Sugar or Powdered Ingredients Sift lightly through a sieve. Measure into a standard measuring cup or spoon and level off with a flat-edge knife or a spatula.

6) Fruits and nuts must be dredged with flour before they are added into a batter. This prevents them from falling to the bottom of a cake.

14

7) In separating eggs, if a bit of yolk drops into the whites, a cloth moistened in cold water and touched to the spilled yolk will pick it up.

8) When beating egg whites do not tap the beater on the edge of the bowl to clear it—the jar of the beater will make the whites lose their fluffiness. Tap the beater on your hand instead.

9) Egg whites for angel or sponge cake beat up lighter and more easily if they are at room temperature. They should be neither too warm nor too cold. Unless the kitchen is unusually warm, remove the eggs from the refrigerator and let them stand at room temperature for two or three hours before they are to be beaten.

10) When using heatproof glass pans, reduce the oven temperature 25° but use the same baking time called for in the recipe.

11) The sides of pans used for small cupcakes should be greased very little because heavy greasing tends to make the batter "turn in" at the top.

12) If directions are followed as to the oven temperature and the size of the pan, the cake should be done in the time specified. But to make sure, always test a cake before removing it from the oven in the following ways:

a) See if the cake has risen well and has a delicately brown crust.

b) If it is a butter cake, see if the cake has shrunk away slightly from the sides of the pan.

c) Press a finger lightly on the cake's surface—it should spring back and leave no imprint.

d) Insert a toothpick or wire tester into the center of the cake—it should come out clean and dry. If any batter clings to the tester the cake is not yet done.

13) If pans are new, butter them well and place them in a moderate oven for 15 minutes. Then wash them and they are ready for use. This treatment prevents cakes from burning in new pans.

14) For easy decoration of a child's birthday cake, press a cookie cutter in the shape of an animal lightly into the icing on top of the cake, to make an outline. Then the outline can be filled with tinted icing from a pastry tube, or with small colored candies, small jelly beans, or chocolate bits.

15) To store a cake, as soon as it is completely cooled, place it in a covered box (as airtight as possible). Set the cake on a large piece of wax paper inside the box; this makes for ease in handling.

Cakes can also be stored in the crisper drawer of the refrigerator where vegetables and fruits are normally stored.

Cakes can be made ahead of time and frozen un-iced in the freezing compartment of the refrigerator. (Frosted cakes can also be frozen, but icings have a more delicate flavor if they are served as soon as they are made.) Remove the cake from the freezer at least six hours before serving and allow it to defrost slowly at room temperature.

To keep a loaf or layer cake fresh after it has been cut, put a slice of fresh bread in the cake box with it, or an apple cut in half. These help to keep the cake moist.

Wrapping the cut cake in plastic wrap or aluminum foil and placing it low in the refrigerator is another easy way to keep cakes fresh and moist.

16) If baking at high altitudes the following adjustments should be made: The baking temperature should be raised about 25°. The leavening (baking powder, soda, or both) at 3500 feet should be decreased by about one-third, at 5000 feet by about one-half, and above 5000 feet by about two-thirds. It is also advisable to beat egg whites somewhat less; keep them soft and fluffy but do not beat them until they are dry.

17) In making applesauce cake, the applesauce is sometimes the only liquid used. But applesauce varies in liquid content, so often a little sweet milk or buttermilk is necessary. And too, sometimes a little more flour may be needed.

TIME AND TEMPERATURE CHART FOR CAKES

Type of Cake	Oven Temperature	Baking Time
Angel Food	350°	35–40 min.
Sponge	325°	60–65 min.
Jelly Roll	375°	12–15 min.
Cup Cakes	375°	15–18 min.
8–9-inch layers	350°	25–30 min.
9-inch square	350°	35–40 min.
13- × 9-inch sheet	350°	35–40 min.
Loaf	350°	55–60 min.
Fruit	300°–375°	1–2 hours

Slow Oven	250°–325°	Hot Oven	400°–450°
Moderate Oven	350°–375°	Very Hot Oven	450°–500°

A CAKE ON WHICH TO PRACTICE

¼ cup (½ stick) butter or margarine

1 egg

1½ cups cake flour, sifted

1 tsp. vanilla

⅔ cup granulated sugar

½ cup milk

2 tsp. baking powder

¼ tsp. salt

Remove the butter from the refrigerator and let it soften. Light the oven, set it to 350° and let it heat up (this takes 10 to 15 minutes).

Grease and flour an 8-inch square baking pan "grease and flour" is explained in the "How To" glossary (p. 8).

Place on the work table all the utensils, etc. that you'll need:

a mixing bowl

2 measuring cups

a measuring teaspoon

a large mixing spoon (wooden)

a wire whisk (or large fork)

a cereal bowl

a flour sieve

a wire cake rack

a spatula

toothpicks (for testing)

Put the softened butter and the sugar in the mixing bowl. Cream these together with the mixing spoon by pressing against the side of the bowl with the back of the spoon. Continue doing this until the butter and sugar are thoroughly combined and the mixture looks creamy (not lumpy or coarsely grained).

Break the egg into the cereal bowl and beat it well with the wire whisk or the large fork. Pour the beaten egg into the creamed butter-sugar mixture and stir it in thoroughly. Add in the vanilla and stir it in completely.

Sift together the flour and the baking powder and the salt through the sieve onto a piece of wax paper. Then sift them again into the mixing bowl on top of the creamed mixture. Now beat the mixture well with the mixing spoon or with a rotary beater or the wire whisk. Be sure all the flour is incorporated.

Pour the batter into the prepared pan and set the pan in the heated oven. Let the cake bake for about 35 minutes.

Test the cake then with the toothpick test (See p. 15) to see if it is done. If it is not, let it continue baking for ten minutes longer and then test it again.

Remove the pan from the oven and let the cake stand in the pan for about 5 minutes. Then gently ease the cake (using a knife or spatula to work around the edges) from the pan and place it on the cake rack until it is completely cool.

Meanwhile prepare the following Pink Frosting and when the cake is cool spread it on top of and on the sides of the cake. (Frosting directions can be found on p. 157).

Pink Frosting

½ **stick butter or margarine**	1 **Tbsp. condensed milk**
2 **cups confectioners sugar,**	1 **tsp. red cake coloring**
sifted	1 **tsp. vanilla**
⅛ **tsp. salt**	

Cream the butter in a mixing bowl with the sugar; add in a small amount of sugar at a time and make the mixture very smooth and creamy. Then add in the salt, the cake coloring, and the milk. Stir thoroughly with your mixing spoon until the frosting is completely smooth.

THREE SPECIAL WARNINGS

1. Do not open oven door during first half of time any cake is baking. This can cause it to fall.

2. In making yeast cakes, be sure to punch down the dough with your fist in between risings.

3. Always wash your beater well before beating egg whites. Rinse it in warm water.

Recipes

❧ Cakes for the Family
Chapter 1

MINTED CHOCOLATE CAKE

1 stick butter	1½ cups cake flour, sifted
1 cup granulated sugar	½ tsp. salt
2 egg yolks	1 tsp. baking soda
2 squares unsweetened choco- late	1 cup sour milk
	1 tsp. vanilla

Beat the butter, sugar and egg yolks until they are creamy. Melt the chocolate and add it to the egg mix.

Sift the flour, salt and soda together and add them into the egg mix alternately with the milk. Mix well, then add the vanilla and stir thoroughly again.

Bake in an 8-inch greased and floured square pan in a 350° oven for 30 to 40 minutes.

Frost with Uncooked Icing (See p. 175), adding ½ tsp. pure peppermint extract to the frosting mix.

LEMON CAKE

½ stick butter	1 tsp. baking powder
1 cup confectioners sugar, sifted	⅔ cup milk
	1 tsp. lemon extract
4 eggs, separated	1 cup granulated sugar
1 cup cake flour, sifted	1 tsp. vinegar

Cream the butter and the confectioners sugar together until they are smooth. Beat well yolks of 3 eggs, add them into the creamed mixture, and beat again.

Sift the flour with the baking powder and add it in alternately with the milk into the creamed mixture. Then put in the extract.

Pour this batter into two greased and floured 8-inch layer cake pans.

Now beat the whites of 4 eggs until they are stiff. Fold in the granulated sugar and the vinegar, and spread this mixture over the batter in the pans.

Bake for 25 minutes in a 350° oven. Put the layers together with Pineapple Egg Yolk Filling (See p. 159), which uses the fourth egg yolk.

THE ETHEL BRANNON CAKE

¾ cup boiling water
½ cup cocoa
1¾ cups cake flour, sifted
1¾ cups granulated sugar
1½ tsp. baking soda
1 tsp. salt

½ cup salad oil
7 egg yolks, unbeaten
2 tsp. vanilla
1 cup egg whites (8 large or 10 small eggs)
½ tsp. cream of tartar

Combine the water and the cocoa; let them cool. Sift the flour, the sugar, soda, and the salt together. Make a well in the flour mix and add the oil, the egg yolks, the cooled cocoa mixture, and the vanilla. Beat until smooth.

Beat the egg whites and cream of tartar together until they are very stiff. Pour the egg yolk mixture in a thin stream over the entire surface of the egg whites, gently cutting in until all is blended.

Pour the batter into an ungreased 10-inch tube pan. Bake in a preheated oven at 325° for 65 to 70 minutes. Invert the pan and let the cake cool.

PEANUT BUTTER CAKE

½ cup peanut butter
1 stick butter
1 cup brown sugar
½ cup granulated sugar
2 eggs, beaten

¾ tsp. vanilla
2½ cups all-purpose flour, sifted
3 tsp. baking powder
½ tsp. salt
1 cup milk

Cream the butter and the peanut butter together. Stir in the sugars and beat well. Add the beaten eggs and the vanilla.

Sift the flour with the baking powder and the salt. Add the flour mix into the batter alternately with the milk.

Pour the batter into a well greased and floured 13 × 9 × 2-inch pan. Bake in a 350° oven for 35 minutes. When the cake is cool, frost it with Uncooked Icing, (See p. 175).

IRISH APPLE CAKE

3 cups cake flour, sifted
¾ cup granulated sugar
½ tsp. salt
3 egg yolks
2 sticks butter, softened

1¾ cups applesauce
½ tsp. cinnamon
¼ tsp. ground cloves
Grated rind of 1 lemon

Heat the oven to 350°. Grease and flour a square 9-inch pan.

Mix the flour, sugar and salt. Add in the egg yolks and the butter. Combine well. Divide the mixture into two parts. Press one portion into the greased pan.

Mix the applesauce, the cinnamon, the cloves, and the lemon rind; spread this on top of the dough in the pan. Spread the rest of the batter over the applesauce.

Bake for 40 to 50 minutes. Top with whipped cream or Lemon Sauce, (See p. 178). Serves 9.

CHOCOLATE FUDGE CAKE

2 cups cake flour, sifted
3 tsp. baking powder
½ tsp. baking soda
¼ tsp. salt
½ cup shortening
1 cup granulated sugar

2 egg yolks, beaten
3 squares unsweetened chocolate, melted
1¼ cups milk
1 tsp. vanilla
2 egg whites, stiffly beaten

Sift the flour once; then measure it. Add the baking powder, the soda, and the salt, and sift three times.

Cream the shortening thoroughly, add in the sugar gradually, then cream them together until they are light and fluffy. Now add the egg yolks and the chocolate, then the flour and the milk alternately, a small amount at a time. Beat after each addition until the mixture is smooth. Add the vanilla and fold in the egg whites.

Bake in two greased and floured 9-inch layer cake pans in a 350° oven for 30 minutes. Put the layers together with Fudge Frosting, (See p. 163).

DELICIOUS HONEY CAKE

½ stick butter	½ tsp. cinnamon
¼ cup shortening	½ tsp. salt
1 cup strained honey	1 tsp. baking soda
1 egg, well beaten	½ cup sour milk
4 cups cake flour, sifted	

Cream together the butter with the shortening. Add in gradually the honey and the beaten egg and blend until the mixture is smooth.

Sift the flour with the cinnamon and the salt. Dissolve the soda in the sour milk. Add into the creamed mixture the flour mixture alternately with the milk. Blend together smoothly.

Bake in a greased and floured shallow 13 × 9-inch pan in a 350° oven for 50 minutes.

When the cake is cool serve it cut into slices or squares.

DELIGHT OATMEAL CAKE

1 stick butter, softened	1 tsp. cinnamon
½ cup granulated sugar	½ tsp. nutmeg
1 cup brown sugar	1 tsp. baking soda
1 tsp. vanilla	1 cup milk
1 egg	1 cup rolled oats
1½ cups all-purpose flour, sifted	(quick or oldfashioned)
½ tsp. salt	1 tsp. baking soda

Heat the oven to 325°. Beat the butter until it is creamy; add the sugars gradually and beat until they are thoroughly blended and smooth. Add in the vanilla and the egg; beat well.

Sift together the flour, salt, soda, and the spices and add them to the creamed mixture alternately with the milk. Stir in the oats.

Pour the batter into a greased and floured 9-inch square pan. Bake in the preheated oven for 40 to 45 minutes. Leave the cake in the pan. Frost it with Nutmeat Coconut Frosting, (See p. 165).

This cake can be served warm or cold.

WHITE BUTTER CAKE

1 stick country or dairy butter	½ cup water
1½ cups granulated sugar	½ cup milk
3 cups cake flour, sifted	1 tsp. vanilla
3 tsp. baking powder	8 drops of almond extract
¼ tsp. salt	4 egg whites

Cream the butter, add in the sugar and cream together until the mix is light.

Sift the flour with the baking powder and the salt. Add about 4 Tbsp. of flour to the creamed mixture, then add the remaining flour and the water and milk alternately. Mix well, but do not overbeat. Add in the extracts. Beat the egg whites until they are stiff and carefully fold them into the batter.

Pour the batter into two greased and floured 8-inch layer cake pans lined with lightly greased wax paper. Bake at 375° for from 25 to 30 minutes.

Ice the cake with a cooked icing of your choice.

CINNAMON PINEAPPLE CAKE

1 stick butter or margarine	2 large eggs
1 tsp. baking soda	2¼ cups cake flour, sifted
½ tsp. salt	½ cup milk
1 tsp. cinnamon	1 cup (8 oz. pkg.) creamed cottage cheese
1⅓ cups light brown sugar, firmly packed	¼ cup crushed pineapple, drained

Soften the butter or margarine and mix it with the soda, the salt, and the cinnamon. Gradually blend in the sugar. Beat in the eggs, one at a time. Add in the flour alternately with the milk, beginning and ending with flour. Stir in the cottage cheese and the pineapple.

Turn the mixture into a well greased, lightly floured 9-inch square shallow pan. Bake in a preheated moderate oven at 350° for 50 minutes, or until a toothpick inserted in the center comes out clean.

Remove the cake from the oven and spread it with Cinnamon Pineapple Topping, (See p. 176). Broil until golden brown (about 20 minutes). Yield: 12 to 16 portions.

WHOLE WHEAT CAKE

1¼ cups all-purpose flour, sifted	½ cup shortening
	¾ cup granulated sugar
2¼ tsp. baking powder	2 eggs, beaten
½ tsp. salt	½ tsp. vanilla
¾ cup whole wheat flour	1 cup milk

Sift the white flour, measure it, and resift it 3 times with the baking powder and the salt. Then add in the whole wheat flour; stir it in thoroughly.

Cream the shortening with the sugar. Add the beaten eggs and beat the mixture until it is smooth. Put in the vanilla. Then add the flour mixture alternately with the milk into the creamed mixture.

Bake in two greased and floured 8-inch layer cake pans lined with lightly greased wax paper, in a 375° oven for about 25 minutes.

Cool the cake in the pans for 5 minutes; then turn it out to cool completely on a cake rack. Serve the cake plain or with your favorite icing or filling, or both.

(from Meta Given's THE MODERN FAMILY COOK BOOK)

DEPENDABLE CAKE

1 heaping Tbsp. butter (a little less than ¼ stick)	1½ cups all-purpose flour, sifted
1 cup granulated sugar	1 tsp. baking powder
1 egg	Pinch of salt
1 tsp. baking soda	1 tsp. vanilla
1 cup buttermilk	1 Tbsp. cocoa

Mix the butter and the sugar together thoroughly. Beat the egg and add it in. Dissolve the soda in the buttermilk; add this into the mixture.

Sift the flour, the baking powder, and the salt together and add them into the first mixture. Now put in the vanilla and the cocoa and mix the batter well.

Bake in a greased and floured 9-inch square pan in a 350° oven for about 30 minutes, or until a toothpick proves the cake is done. Top with One Minute Fudge Icing, (See p. 174).

JELLY ROLL CAKE

1 cup cake flour, sifted	3 eggs, well beaten
2 tsp. baking powder	6 Tbsp. hot water
1 cup granulated sugar	1 cup jelly

Sift the flour, sugar and baking powder together. Add in the eggs, then the hot water. Mix well.

Spread the batter about $\frac{1}{4}$ inch thick on a large lightly greased and floured jelly roll pan, $15\frac{1}{2} \times 10\frac{1}{2} \times 1$-inch, that has been lined with lightly greased wax paper. Bake for 12 to 15 minutes in a 400° oven.

When the cake is done, turn it out while hot onto a large sheet of wax paper dusted with powdered sugar. Beat up the jelly with a fork and spread it on the cake quickly while the cake is warm. Trim off all the crust around the edges, and roll the cake by lifting up one end of the paper and gradually rolling the cake over and over.

Wrap the paper around the cake, then roll it in a clean cloth until it is cool. Before serving the cake, if desired, sprinkle powdered sugar over the cake.

LEMON MERINGUE CAKE

½ stick butter	1 tsp. lemon extract
½ cup granulated sugar	½ tsp. salt
3 egg yolks, beaten	1 tsp. vanilla
6 Tbsp. milk	1 tsp. baking powder
1 cup cake flour, sifted	

Cream the butter with the sugar thoroughly. Add in the rest of the ingredients and beat for three minutes.

Pour the batter into a shallow greased and floured 8-inch square pan, lined with lightly greased wax paper. Bake for 20 minutes in a moderate oven at 350°.

Finish the cake with Lemon Meringue Topping, (See p. 177).

APPLESAUCE CAKE, NO. 2 (with Walnuts)

2 cups all-purpose flour, sifted	¼ tsp. ground cloves
	½ cup shortening
1 cup granulated sugar	1 egg (or 2 yolks, beaten)
½ tsp. salt	1 cup thick, smooth applesauce
1 tsp. baking soda	
½ tsp. cinnamon	1 cup chopped walnuts
½ tsp. nutmeg	

Heat the oven to 350°.

Measure the flour, sugar, salt, soda, and the spices with the shortening into a bowl; beat with a spoon or electric mixer until the mix is fluffy. Add the egg and beat again. Stir in the applesauce, beating until the total mixture is smooth. Then stir in the walnuts.

Bake in a greased and floured 9 × 5 × 3-inch pan for 50 or 60 minutes. Let the cake stand in the pan for 10 minutes, then turn it out on a cake rack.

BLACK DEVIL'S CAKE (Sugarless)

½ cup shortening	½ tsp. baking soda
½ cup molasses	½ tsp. salt
2 eggs, well beaten	1½ tsp. baking powder
2 squares unsweetened chocolate, melted	1 cup milk
	1 tsp. vanilla
1¾ cups cake flour, sifted	

Cream the shortening with the molasses; add the eggs and the chocolate. Blend well.

Sift the flour, soda, salt, and baking powder together and stir them into the creamed mix alternately with the milk. Add the vanilla. Then pour the batter into two greased and floured 8-inch layer cake pans.

Bake at 350° for 20 minutes, or until the cake proves to be done when tested with a toothpick. Ice with your favorite icing.

ORANGE RAISIN CAKE

1 cup granulated sugar	1 whole orange
1 stick butter	1 cup raisins
2 cups all-purpose flour, sifted	1 tsp. soda
	1 cup buttermilk
Pinch of salt	1 egg

Cream together the sugar and the butter. Sift the flour twice with the salt, then stir it in with the sugar and butter.

Grind the orange and raisins through a food chopper (or chop up thoroughly by hand). Add all except 1 Tbsp. to the butter-flour mixture. Add the soda to the buttermilk and combine this into the mix. Stir in the egg. Blend well together with a spoon (do not use an electric beater).

Bake in a 10 × 6-inch greased and floured loaf pan at 350° for 45 to 50 minutes.

Ice with Creamy Smooth Icing, (See p. 172) to which the 1 Tbsp. of the ground orange-raisins should be added.

NUTTY APPLE CAKE

2 cups granulated sugar	1 tsp. baking soda
½ cup shortening	½ tsp. salt
2 eggs, separated	1 tsp. cinnamon
1 tsp. vanilla	1 tsp. nutmeg
2 cups all-purpose flour, sifted	4 cups chopped tart apples
	1 cup chopped pecan meats

Cream together the sugar and the shortening. Beat the egg yolks well and add them in. Add in the vanilla.

Sift the flour, soda, salt, and the spices together and combine them into the moist mixture. Fold in the apples and the pecan meats. Blend well. Now beat the egg white stiffly and fold them in.

Bake in a greased and floured 12 × 8 × 2-inch pan, at 300° for about 1 hour.

SWISS CHOCOLATE CAKE

2 cups cake flour, sifted
½ tsp. salt
2½ tsp. baking powder
1 stick butter
1¼ cups granulated sugar
1 tsp. vanilla

2 egg yolks
1 cup milk
¾ cup unsweetened chocolate, grated
2 egg whites, stiffly beaten

Sift together the flour, salt, and the baking powder. In a mixing bowl put the butter, sugar, and the vanilla, and beat in the egg yolks until the mixture is light and fluffy. Add in the flour mixture alternately with the milk. Beat the mixture until it is smooth, then add the chocolate, mixing it in thoroughly. Now fold in the egg whites.

Pour the batter into two greased and floured 8-inch layer cake pans. Bake for 25 minutes in a 375° oven. Take the layers out of the oven when they are done and let them set in the pans for 5 minutes before turning them out onto a cake rack.

Cool the cake thoroughly before frosting it with Uncooked Icing, (See p. 175).

DRIED APRICOT CAKE

1 cup dried apricots
2 cups water
6 Tbsp. granulated sugar
½ cup shortening
1 cup granulated sugar
2 egg yolks

1 tsp. vanilla
1¾ cups cake flour, sifted
½ tsp. salt
1 tsp. baking powder
½ tsp. baking soda
¼ cup water

Simmer the apricots with 2 cups of water and 6 Tbsp. of sugar for 30 minutes on top of the stove. Drain off the liquid and mash the fruit. Measure out ¼ cup of pulp.

Cream the shortening with 1 cup of sugar thoroughly; add in the egg yolks and the vanilla. Beat well.

Sift together the flour, salt, soda, and the baking powder, and add them alternately to the egg mixture with ¼ cup of water and the apricot pulp.

Bake in an 8-inch greased and floured square pan lined with lightly greased wax paper at 350° for 45 minutes.

SILVER WHITE CAKE

2½ cups cake flour, sifted	1 stick butter, softened
1⅓ cups granulated sugar	1 tsp. vanilla
½ tsp. salt	1 cup milk
2½ tsp. baking powder	3 egg whites

Heat oven to 350°. Grease and flour two 8-inch layer cake pans, or an oblong pan, 13 × 9 × 2 inches.

Sift the flour, sugar, salt, and the baking powder into a bowl. Add the butter, the vanilla, and ⅔ cup of the milk. Beat for 2 minutes. Add the balance of the milk and the egg whites. Beat 2 minutes more, vigorously. Pour the batter into the prepared pans.

Bake in layers for 30 to 35 minutes, the oblong cake about 35 minutes. Allow the cake to cool. Fill with your favorite lemon filling. Frost with a white icing. Sprinkle grated coconut on top.

MOTHER SANFORD'S SPECIAL CAKE

1½ cups soft brown sugar	½ tsp. salt
½ cup shortening	1 tsp. cinnamon
2 eggs, beaten	½ tsp. ground cloves
½ cup molasses	½ tsp. allspice
½ cup milk	¼ cup dates, chopped
2 cups all-purpose flour, sifted	½ cup seedless raisins
1½ tsp. baking powder	¼ cup chopped maraschino cherries

Cream the sugar and the shortening together thoroughly. Blend in the beaten eggs. Add the molasses and the milk and mix thoroughly.

Sift the flour with the baking powder, the salt, and the spices. Dredge the fruits with a little of the flour. Add the sifted flour and the floured fruits into the creamed molasses mixture and mix together well.

Bake in a greased and floured 9-inch tube pan at 350° for 55 minutes to 1 hour.

When the cake has cooled, frost with Snow White Frosting, (See p. 167).

GRANDMA'S MOLASSES CAKE

⅔ cup shortening
¼ cup granulated sugar
¾ cup unsulphured molasses
2 cups all-purpose flour,
                      sifted

½ tsp. baking soda
¾ tsp. salt
1¼ tsp. baking powder
2 eggs
½ cup milk

Cream the shortening with the sugar. Add in the molasses slowly; beat well.

Sift together the flour, soda, salt, and the baking powder; add one-half of this into the molasses mix. Now add in the eggs and beat again. Add in the rest of the dry ingredients alternately with the milk.

Bake in an 8-inch greased and floured square pan at 325° for about 1 hour.

MOLASSES LAYER CAKE

⅞ stick butter
1 cup granulated sugar
1 egg, beaten
3 Tbsp. molasses
1 tsp. baking soda
¾ cup sour milk

1 tsp. vanilla
2 cups all-purpose flour,
                      sifted
¼ tsp. salt
1 tsp. baking powder

Cream the butter, the sugar and the egg together thoroughly. Add in the molasses and mix well. Dissolve the soda in the sour milk and add in the vanilla.

Sift the flour with the salt and the baking powder. Sift the flour mix into the creamed mixture alternately with the sour milk mix.

Divide the batter into two greased and floured 9-inch layer cake pans and bake in a 350° oven for 25 to 30 minutes.

Cool the layers and put them together with Peanut Brittle Filling, (See p. 159).

SPICED COFFEE LAYER CAKE

½ cup shortening	¼ tsp. salt
1 cup granulated sugar	1 tsp. cinnamon
2 eggs, separated	1 tsp. nutmeg
2 cups cake flour, sifted	½ cup strong coffee
2 tsp. baking powder	

Cream the shortening; add in the sugar gradually. Cream them well together. Add in the egg yolks and beat well.

Sift the flour, baking powder, salt, and the spices together. Add these alternately with the coffee into the first mixture. Beat the egg whites stiffly and fold them in.

Bake in 2 greased and floured 9-inch layer cake pans in a 350° oven for 25 to 30 minutes.

Spread with Mocha Frosting, (See p. 164).

COCONUT GOLD CAKE

1⅞ cups cake flour, sifted	1 tsp. lemon extract
1¼ cups granulated sugar	1 tsp. vanilla
¾ tsp. salt	¾ stick butter
3 tsp. baking powder	4 egg yolks
1 cup milk	

Sift the flour, sugar, salt, and the baking powder together in a bowl. Mix the milk and the flavorings in another bowl. Pour half of the milk mixture into the flour mix and beat well.

Cream together the butter and the egg yolks in a small bowl; beat about 2 minutes. Add the balance of the milk into the flour-milk mixture, then add in the egg yolk mix. Beat thoroughly.

Separate the batter into 2 greased and floured 8-inch layer cake pans. Bake at 350° for 25 to 30 minutes. When the layers have cooled, ice with Coconut Frosting, (See p. 161).

SURPRISE CAKE

1½ cups granulated sugar	2 Tbsp. cocoa
¾ cup shortening	½ tsp. nutmeg
3 eggs	½ tsp. cinnamon
1¾ cups cake flour, sifted	¾ cup sour milk
½ tsp. baking soda	½ tsp. lemon extract
½ tsp. salt	½ cup nut meats, chopped

Cream the sugar and the shortening together thoroughly. Stir in the eggs.

Sift the flour with the soda, salt, cocoa and spices, and add it to the creamed mixture alternately with the sour milk. Blend in the extract and the nuts. Beat thoroughly.

Bake at 350° in an 8-inch greased and floured square pan for 40 to 50 minutes. Frost with Surprise Frosting, (See p. 168).

QUICK CAKE

2½ cups cake flour, sifted	½ cup shortening, softened
1½ cups granulated sugar	1 cup milk
3 tsp. baking powder	2 eggs
1 tsp. salt	2 tsp. vanilla

Preheat the oven to 350°. Grease and flour two 9-inch layer cake pans.

Sift the flour, sugar, baking powder and the salt into a mixing bowl. Add the shortening and ¾ cup of milk. Beat until the flour is dampened. Then beat faster for 2 minutes. Add the eggs and vanilla and ¼ cup of milk and beat for 1 minute.

Pour the batter into the prepared pans. With a spatula cut through the batter several times to remove air bubbles.

Bake at 350° for 25 to 30 minutes. Cool the pans on a rack for 10 minutes. Then remove the layers from the pans and continue to cool them until they are cold. Frost to taste.

COCOA COCONUT CAKE

2 cups all-purpose flour, sifted	1½ cups granulated sugar
1½ tsp. baking soda	2 eggs, beaten
¼ tsp. salt	1 tsp. vanilla
⅔ cup cocoa	½ cup buttermilk
⅔ cup shortening	½ cup boiling water

Sift the flour, soda, salt, and the cocoa together 3 times.

Cream the shortening until it is soft. Add in the sugar and blend thoroughly. Add the beaten eggs and beat vigorously until the mixture is smooth and fluffy. Stir in the vanilla.

Now add in the flour mixture alternately with the buttermilk in 3 or 4 portions, beginning and ending with a flour insertion, and beating well after each addition. Add the boiling water all at once and stir until the batter is smooth.

Pour the batter into two greased and floured 8-inch layer cake pans. Bake in a 350° oven for 30 minutes or until the cake tests done. Turn the cake out on rack to cool.

Frost with Nutmeat Coconut Frosting, (See p. 165). Serves 10.

(From Meta Given's MODERN FAMILY COOK BOOK)

GRAHAM CRACKER CAKE

½ cup shortening	¼ tsp. salt
1 cup granulated sugar	1½ tsp. baking powder
3 eggs, separated	¾ cup milk
½ tsp. vanilla	30 graham crackers, crushed fine
¼ cup all-purpose flour, sifted	½ cup pecans, chopped

Cream the shortening with the sugar thoroughly. Add in the egg yolks and the vanilla and beat well.

Sift the flour with the salt and the baking powder. Add the sifted flour into the creamed mixture alternately with the milk and the crushed crumbs.

Beat the egg whites lightly and fold them into the batter. Lastly, add in the nuts.

Bake in two lightly greased and floured 8-inch layer cake pans, lined with lightly greased wax paper, for 25 minutes at 350°. Frost to taste.

BUTTERMILK CAKE

1 stick butter	½ tsp. baking soda
1 cup granulated sugar	½ cup buttermilk
1½ cups cake flour, sifted	½ tsp. vanilla
½ tsp. cream of tartar	3 egg whites
¼ tsp. salt	

Cream the butter; add the sugar gradually; cream continually.

Sift the flour with the cream of tartar, the salt, and the soda. Add it into the creamed mixture, a little at a time, alternately with the buttermilk. Then add in the vanilla.

Beat the egg whites stiffly and fold them into the batter.

Turn the batter into two greased and floured 8-inch layer cake pans or one medium-size loaf pan. Bake at 350° for 25 to 30 minutes (slightly longer if the loaf pan is used).

When the cake has cooled, frost with Creamy Smooth Icing, (See p. 172).

COCONUT JELLY CAKE

2 cups all-purpose flour, sifted	1⅜ sticks butter, softened
1¼ cups granulated sugar	2 eggs
3 tsp. baking powder	1 tsp. vanilla
¼ tsp. salt	¾ cup jelly
⅔ cup milk	1½ cups shredded coconut

Sift the flour before measuring, then resift it with the sugar, baking powder, and the salt. Make a hollow in the center of the flour mixture and add the milk, the butter, the eggs, and the vanilla. Beat well until the mixture is smooth.

Pour the batter into two greased and floured 9-inch layer cake pans. Bake about 20 minutes at 375°. Let the cake stand in the pans for five minutes before turning it out.

When the cake is cool, slice the layers horizontally with a sharp knife. Just before serving it, spread the cake layers with the jelly and sprinkle on each equal portions of the coconut. Then put the layers together.

Light as Air—Angel, Sponge and Chiffon
Chapter 2

FEATHERWEIGHT CAKE NO. 1

2½ cups cake flour, sifted
3½ tsp. baking powder
½ tsp. salt
1¾ cups granulated sugar
¾ cup shortening

1⅛ cups milk
1 tsp. almond or vanilla
                    extract
⅔ cups egg whites, unbeaten
    (6 large or 8 small eggs)

Sift together the flour, baking powder, salt and sugar. Add the shortening and the milk. Beat for 2 minutes. Add the flavoring and the egg whites and beat for 2 minutes more.

Pour the batter into two 8-inch greased and floured layer cake pans and bake at 350° for 35 to 40 minutes.

Frost with Hula Frosting, (See p. 163).

YELLOW CHIFFON CAKE

2 eggs, separated
1½ cups granulated sugar
2½ cups cake flour, sifted
3 tsp. baking powder

1 tsp. salt
⅓ cup cooking oil
1 cup milk
1 tsp. vanilla

Heat oven to 350°; grease well and flour two round 9-inch layer cake pans, or an oblong pan, 13 × 9 × 2-inches.

Beat the egg whites until they are foamy. Gradually beat in ½ cup of sugar. Continue beating until the mixture is very stiff and glossy.

Sift the remaining sugar, the flour, baking powder and salt into another bowl. Add in the oil, half of the milk, and the vanilla. Beat for 1 minute with a mixer at medium speed or 150 vigorous strokes by hand. Add the remaining milk and the egg yolks. Beat for 1 more minute. Fold in the egg white meringue.

Pour the batter into the prepared pans. Bake the cake in the layer pans for 25 to 30 minutes, in the oblong pan, for 40 to 50 minutes. Frost with Chocolate Butter Icing, (See p. 171).

ORANGE SPONGE CAKE

2 egg yolks, unbeaten	2 egg whites, stiffly beaten
¾ cup granulated sugar	1 cup cake flour, sifted
¼ tsp. grated orange rind	¼ tsp. baking soda
4 Tbsp. orange juice	¼ tsp. salt
½ tsp. lemon juice	

Grease and flour a 9-inch tube pan or deep round tin and line it with greased wax paper.

Put the egg yolks, the sugar, orange rind, orange juice and lemon juice in a mixing bowl and mix well. Fold in the beaten egg whites. Then after sifting the flour, baking soda and salt together four times, combine them in the mixing bowl with the other ingredients. Beat well.

Pour the batter into the pan and bake for 30 minutes at 375°.

The cake may be frosted or it may be sliced into layers and filled with orange marmalade or a cooked orange filling.

YELLOW ANGEL FOOD CAKE

1½ cups cake flour, sifted	½ cup orange juice, pulp and grated rind combined
½ tsp. salt	
½ tsp. baking powder	1½ cups granulated sugar
5 eggs, separated	¾ tsp. cream of tartar
	1 tsp. lemon extract

Sift the flour, salt and baking powder together. Beat the egg yolks until they are thick and lemon colored. Add the orange juice, the pulp and the grated rind. Beat until the mixture is light and fluffy. Gradually beat in the sugar. Fold in the dry ingredients.

Beat the egg whites with the cream of tartar until they are stiff but not dry. Fold them in the egg yolk batter and then add the lemon extract.

Bake in a 10-inch ungreased tube pan in a 325° oven for about 1 hour. Invert the pan until the cake is cool.

Ice with Orange Icing, (See p. 174).

CHIFFON CAKE

1 cup egg whites (8 large or 10 small eggs)
½ tsp. cream of tartar
2 cups cake flour, sifted
1½ cups granulated sugar, sifted
1 tsp. salt

3 tsp. baking powder
½ cup cooking oil
4 egg yolks
¾ cup water
1 tsp. vanilla
2 tsp. grated lemon rind

Preheat oven to 325°.

Beat the egg whites and cream of tartar together until very stiff peaks are formed. Sift the flour, sugar, salt and baking powder together in a large mixing bowl. Make a well in the center of the flour and add the oil, egg yolks and water. Beat with a wooden spoon until the mixture is smooth. Stir in the vanilla and the grated rind.

Gradually pour the egg yolk mixture over the beaten whites, folding in gently with a rubber spatula just until everything is blended. Do not stir.

Pour the batter into an ungreased 10-inch tube cake pan at once. Bake 1 hour at 325° or 50 minutes at 350°. Immediately turn the pan upside down to cool the cake. When it is cool, gently ease the cake from the sides of the pan with a knife. Lift out the cake and invert it on a plate.

FEATHERWEIGHT CAKE, NO. 2

½ cup shortening
1 cup granulated sugar
2 cups cake flour, sifted
2 tsp. baking powder

½ tsp. salt
⅔ cup milk
3 egg whites
1 tsp. vanilla

Cream together the shortening and the sugar. Mix and sift three times the flour, baking powder, and the salt; add these alternately with the milk into the first mixture.

Beat the egg whites stiffly and fold them in. Add the vanilla and turn the batter into two greased and floured 9-inch layer cake pans. Bake at 350° for 20 to 30 minutes.

Frost with Snow White Frosting, with coconut added, (See p. 167).

SYRUP ANGEL FOOD CAKE

¾ cup white syrup	¼ tsp. salt
1 cup egg whites (8 large or 10 small eggs)	¾ tsp. almond extract
	1 cup cake flour, sifted
1 tsp. cream of tartar	½ cup granulated sugar

Boil the syrup until it forms a soft ball in cold water. Beat the egg whites until they are frothy, then add to them the cream of tartar and the salt. Continue beating until the whites are stiff but not dry. Add the hot syrup, a little at a time, beating well after each addition. Add the almond extract.

Sift together the flour and the sugar. Fold this mix into the egg whites and the syrup mixture, blending lightly.

Bake in an ungreased 10-inch tube pan for 60 minutes as follows: first 15 minutes at 320°, then 45 minutes at 300°. When the cake is baked, remove the pan from the oven and invert it for 1 hour before removing the cake from the pan.

HOT MILK SPONGE CAKE

4 eggs	¼ stick butter
2 cups granulated sugar	2 cups all-purpose flour, sifted
½ tsp. salt	
2 tsp. vanilla	2 tsp. baking powder
1 cup milk	

Set the oven at 350°. Grease and flour a 13 × 9-inch pan. In a large mixing bowl beat the eggs with a rotary beater or electric mixer until they are very light. Beat in the sugar, salt and vanilla.

Heat the milk and melt the butter in it. Then beat the hot butter and milk into the egg mixture.

Sift together the flour and baking powder and beat them into the wet mixture very quickly.

Pour the batter immediately into the prepared pan. Bake for 25 to 30 minutes, or until the cake tests done when probed with a toothpick. Top with Broiled Icing, (See p. 169).

DARK CHOCOLATE ANGEL FOOD CAKE

¾ **cup all-purpose flour**	¼ **tsp. baking soda**
4 **Tbsp. cocoa**	½ **tsp. baking powder**
1¼ **cups egg whites (10 large or 13 small eggs)**	1¼ **cups granulated sugar, sifted**
¼ **tsp. salt**	1 **tsp. vanilla**

Sift the flour once; measure it; add the cocoa and sift three more times. Beat the egg whites and the salt until they are foamy, add the soda and baking powder and beat until the eggs will just hold a peak, but are not dry. Fold in the sugar carefully, two tablespoons at a time. Fold in the vanilla. Sift a small amount of flour over the mixture and fold it in carefully; continue to add flour gradually until all the flour is incorporated.

Pour the batter into an ungreased 10-inch tube pan. Bake for one hour, the first 30 minutes at 275°, the next 15 minutes at 300° and the last 15 minutes at 325°. Remove the pan from the oven and invert it until the cake is cool. Then remove the cake from the pan.

EASY METHOD ANGEL FOOD CAKE

1 **cup cake flour, sifted**	1 **cup egg whites (8 large or 10 small eggs)**
1¼ **cups granulated sugar**	
½ **tsp. salt**	1 **tsp. cream of tartar**
	1 **tsp. vanilla**

Sift together four or five times the flour, sugar and one-half the salt. Beat the egg whites with the other half of the salt until they are frothy, then add in the cream of tartar; beat until the whites are light but not dry. Fold the dry ingredients very carefully into the beaten egg whites. When the mixture is partly blended, add in the vanilla. (Be very careful when blending the dry ingredients with the eggs. Use the folding method.)

Bake in an ungreased 9-inch tube pan at 325° for 1 hour.

COFFEE ANGEL CAKE

1⅞ cups granulated sugar	2 Tbsp. water
1 Tbsp. instant coffee	2 tsp. cream of tartar
1½ cups cake flour, sifted	1 tsp. rum extract
½ tsp. salt	1 drop red food coloring
1½ cups egg whites (12 large or 15 small eggs)	

Sift 1 cup of sugar and the instant coffee with the flour four times.

Add the salt to the egg whites and beat until they are foamy. Beat in the water, the cream of tartar, the rum extract and the red food coloring. Continue beating until the egg white mixture is light and stiff but not dry. Then gradually beat in the remaining ⅞ cup of sugar. Using a wire whisk, carefully fold in the sifted sugar and flour. When the batter is thoroughly blended, pour it into an ungreased 10-inch tube pan.

Bake at 375° for 45 minutes. Invert the pan, letting it hang until the cake is cool. Remove the cake from the pan and frost it with Scotch Coffee Icing, (See p. 174).

THREE EGG SPONGE CAKE

1 cup cake flour, sifted	1 cup granulated sugar
1 tsp. baking powder	2 tsp. lemon juice
¼ tsp. salt	6 Tbsp. hot milk
3 eggs	

Sift the flour once, measure it, add the baking powder and the salt, and sift them together three times.

Beat the eggs until they are very thick and light and nearly white (5 to 7 min.). Add in the sugar gradually, beating constantly. Add the lemon juice. Fold in the flour mix, a small amount at a time. Add the milk, mixing quickly until the batter is blended.

Bake in an ungreased 9-inch tube pan at 350° for about 35 minutes. Remove the pan from the oven and invert it for 1 hour, or until the cake is cold.

CREOLE CHIFFON CAKE

¾ cup boiling water
½ cup cocoa
1 Tbsp. instant coffee
1½ cups cake flour, sifted
1¾ cups granulated sugar
4 tsp. baking powder
1 tsp. ground cloves

1 tsp. salt
½ cup cooking oil
7 egg yolks, unbeaten
1 tsp. vanilla
1 cup egg whites (8 large or 10 small)
½ tsp. cream of tartar

Heat the oven to 325°. Stir the water, the cocoa and the coffee together until the mix is smooth. Set it aside to cool.

Sift the flour, sugar, baking powder, cloves and salt into a bowl. Make a well and add the oil, the egg yolks, the cooled cocoa mix, and the vanilla. Beat with a spoon until the mixture is smooth.

Measure the egg whites and the cream of tartar into a large mixing bowl. Beat with an electric beater on high speed for 3 to 5 minutes, or by hand until the whites form very stiff peaks. Pour the egg yolk mixture gradually over the beaten egg whites, folding in just until blended. Do not stir.

Pour the batter into an ungreased 10 × 4-inch tube pan. Bake in the preheated oven for 55 minutes, then increase the oven temperature to 350° and bake 10 or 15 minutes longer. Turn the pan upside down with the tube over the neck of a funnel or bottle. Let it hang until the cake is cold.

Loosen the cake from the sides and tube of the pan with a spatula. Ice the cake with a fluffy white cooked icing flavored with 1 tsp. instant coffee. Decorate it if you wish with melted chocolate spooned over the icing at random.

SUGARLESS ANGEL CAKE

6 egg whites
Pinch of salt
½ tsp. instant coffee
½ tsp. cream of tartar

1 grain saccharin tablet, powdered
½ cup cake flour, sifted
1 tsp. vanilla
¼ tsp. almond extract

Beat the egg whites with the salt, the powdered coffee, the cream of tartar, and the saccharin, until they are high and stiff but not dry. Fold in the flour gradually. Then add in the vanilla and almond flavoring.

Bake in a slow oven at 300° for about 35 minutes in an ungreased 8-inch round pan.

This cake can be frosted with whipped non-fat milk sweetened with saccharin.

BURNT SUGAR CHIFFON CAKE

½ cup burnt sugar mixture
made from
1 cup granulated sugar
½ cup boiling water
2 cups cake flour, sifted
3 tsp. baking powder
1 tsp. salt
1½ cups granulated sugar

½ cup cooking oil
7 egg yolks, unbeaten
¼ cup cold water
1 tsp. vanilla
1 cup egg whites (8 large or
10 small eggs)
½ tsp. cream of tartar

First prepare the burnt sugar mixture by melting 1 cup of sugar in a heavy skillet until it is brown, then pouring in the boiling water. Set this aside.

Sift together the flour, baking powder, salt, and 1½ cups of sugar. Make a well in this and add the oil, the unbeaten egg yolks, one-half of the burnt sugar mixture, the cold water, and the vanilla. Beat well. (The rest of the burnt sugar mixture will be used in the icing.)

Whip the egg whites and cream of tartar together into very stiff peaks; gently fold them into the batter until they are blended. Do not stir.

Pour the batter into an ungreased 10 × 4-inch tube pan immediately, and bake for 65 minutes at 325°. Frost with Burnt Sugar Icing, (See p. 170).

LEMON LIGHT SPONGE CAKE NO. 1

6 eggs, separated
1½ cups granulated sugar
1½ cups cake flour, sifted
½ tsp. salt

6 Tbsp. cold water
1 tsp. lemon extract
1 tsp. grated lemon rind
1½ tsp. baking powder

Beat the egg yolks until they are thick and lemon colored. Gradually beat in the sugar. Sift the flour and salt together and add them alternately with the water to the first mixture. Add the lemon extract and the rind.

Whip the egg whites until they are foamy; add the baking powder and continue whipping until stiff peaks are formed. Fold the whites into the egg yolk mixture.

Pour the batter into an ungreased 9-inch tube pan; bake at 325° for 50 to 60 minutes. When it is cool, cut the cake from the tube and sides of pan, lift out the cake by the tube, and invert it onto a plate.

LEMON LIGHT SPONGE CAKE NO. 2

1 cup cake flour, sifted	5 eggs, separated
1 cup granulated sugar, sifted	1½ Tbsp. lemon juice
1½ tsp. grated lemon rind	¼ tsp. salt
2 Tbsp. water	½ tsp. cream of tartar

Sift the flour once, measure it, and sift again four times.

Add ½ cup of sugar, the lemon rind, and the water to the egg yolks and beat with a rotary beater until they are very thick and light. Add the lemon juice gradually, beating constantly. Add the flour all at once, then stir until it is just blended.

Beat the egg whites and the salt with a rotary beater or whisk. When they become foamy, add the cream of tartar and beat until the mix is stiff enough to hold up in peaks but is not dry. Add the remaining ½ cup of sugar, about 2 Tbsp. at a time, beating well with the beater or whisk. Fold the egg white mix into the egg yolk mixture gently.

Turn the batter into an ungreased 9-inch tube pan. Cut gently through the batter with a knife, to remove air bubbles. Bake in a slow oven at 325° for 1 hour, or until the cake tests done when probed with a toothpick. Remove the pan from the oven and invert it for 1 hour, or until the cake is cold.

SUPREME ANGEL CAKE

1 cup cake flour, sifted	⅓ tsp. salt
1½ cups confectioners sugar, sifted	1 tsp. vanilla
	¼ tsp. almond extract
1½ cups egg whites (12)	1 cup granulated sugar
1½ tsp. cream of tartar	

Measure and sift together three times the flour and the confectioners sugar.

Measure into a large mixing bowl the egg whites, the cream of tartar, salt, vanilla, and the almond extract. Beat with a wire whisk until this mix is foamy. Gradually add in the granulated sugar, 2 Tbsp. at a time. Continue beating until the mixture holds stiff peaks. Sift gradually the flour-sugar mixture over the egg white mix. Fold in gently, just until the flour-sugar disappears.

Place the batter in an ungreased 10-inch tube pan, 4 inches deep. Gently cut through the batter with a knife. Bake at 350° for 35 to 40 minutes. When the cake tests done, invert it in the pan. Let it stand until it is cold. (If desired, a few drops of red food coloring may be added to the batter to tint it a delicate pink.)

CHERRY ANGEL FOOD CAKE

1 cup egg whites (8 large or 10 small eggs)	1½ cups granulated sugar
1 cup cake flour, sifted	½ tsp. almond extract
1 tsp. cream of tartar	¾ tsp. vanilla
¼ tsp. salt	⅓ cup maraschino cherries, sliced and chopped

Beat the egg whites until they are foamy. Sift the flour with the cream of tartar and the salt and add them into the eggs. Beat well. Fold in the sugar gradually. Add the flavorings.

Pour half of the batter into an ungreased 9-inch tube pan. Sprinkle on half the cherries, then add the remainder of the batter and drop the remaining cherries on top.

Bake for 50 minutes at 325° in a preheated oven. Invert the cake immediately and carefully on a cake rack. Allow the cake to hang until it cools and pulls away from the pan.

Coffee Cakes
Chapter 3

STREUSEL FILLED COFFEE CAKE

1½ cups all-purpose flour,
                       sifted
3 tsp. baking powder
¼ tsp. salt
¾ cup granulated sugar

¼ cup shortening
1 egg, well beaten
¼ cup milk
1 tsp. vanilla

Streusel Filling

½ cup brown sugar
2 Tbsp. flour
2 tsp. cinnamon

¼ stick butter, melted
½ cup chopped nuts

Make the filling first. Mix the sugar, flour, and cinnamon together. Blend in the butter and the nut meats. Set aside.

Sift the flour, baking powder, salt, and the sugar together. Cut in the shortening. Mix the egg with the milk and blend them in. Add the vanilla and beat just enough to mix well.

Pour half the batter into a 10 × 6-inch greased and floured loaf pan. Sprinkle on half the filling. Add the remaining batter and then the rest of the filling on top. Bake for 25 to 30 minutes at 375°.

47

COFFEE SPICE CAKE

2 sticks butter
2 cups granulated sugar
4 egg yolks, beaten
1 cup (4 oz.) bitter chocolate, grated
2 cups cake flour, sifted
½ tsp. salt

3 tsp. baking powder
1 tsp. cinnamon
¼ tsp. nutmeg
¼ tsp. ground cloves
1 cup strong cold coffee
4 egg whites, beaten
½ cup almonds, chopped

Cream the butter, add the sugar, then cream them together. Add in the well-beaten egg yolks and the grated chocolate.

Measure the sifted flour, then sift it again with the salt, the baking powder and the spices. Add these dry ingredients to the moist mixture, alternately with the coffee. Fold in the stiffly beaten egg whites, and then the nuts.

Grease and flour two 8-inch square cake pans. Pour in the batter and bake at 350–375° for 45 minutes to an hour. Makes 2 cakes.

APPLE RAISIN COFFEE CAKE

1 cup all-purpose flour, sifted
3 tsp. baking powder
½ tsp. salt
1 tsp. cinnamon
¼ tsp. ground cloves
¼ tsp. nutmeg

¼ cup granulated sugar, plus 3 Tbsp. more
1 cup whole bran cereal
1 cup sweetened applesauce
1 egg
¼ cup vegetable oil
½ cup seedless raisins

Sift together the flour, baking powder, salt, ½ teaspoon cinnamon, the cloves, nutmeg, and ¼ cup of sugar.

Combine the bran cereal with the applesauce, the egg, the oil, and the raisins. Let the mixture stand until most of the moisture is taken up (about 5 minutes). Beat well. Add the sifted dry ingredients, stirring only until they are combined. Spread the batter into a greased and floured 8-inch square pan.

Combine 3 Tbsp. of sugar and ½ tsp. cinnamon; sprinkle this evenly over the batter.

Bake in a hot oven at 400° for about 35 minutes, or until the cake tests done by the toothpick test.

LEMON NUT COFFEE CAKE

2¾ cups all-purpose flour, sifted

3 Tbsp. baking powder

½ tsp. baking soda

½ tsp. salt

½ cup chopped nutmeats

¼ cup shortening, softened

1½ cups granulated sugar

2 eggs

1½ tsp. grated lemon rind

¼ cup lemon juice

¾ cup milk

1½ cups bran flakes

Sift together the flour, baking powder, soda, and the salt. Combine in the nutmeats.

Cream the shortening with the sugar, then add the eggs and the lemon rind. Beat well. Stir in the lemon juice and the milk. Next add in the bran flakes. Then add the sifted dry ingredients, stirring only until they are combined.

Spread the batter in a greased and floured 10 × 6-inch loaf pan. Bake in a 350° oven for about 50 minutes. Cool before slicing.

GOLDEN SAFFRON COFFEE RING

1 pkg. active dry yeast

or

1 cake compressed yeast

½ cup warm water

⅓ cup milk

3 cups all-purpose flour, sifted

6 eggs, slightly beaten

Pinch of saffron, ground

1½ sticks butter, melted

¼ cup granulated sugar

¾ tsp. salt

Sliced blanched almonds

Sliced candied red and green cherries

Golden raisins

Dissolve the yeast in the warm water (lukewarm for the compressed yeast) in a large bowl. Stir in the milk, flour, eggs and saffron. Beat together with a wooden spoon for about 6 minutes, or until the dough is elastic. Stir in the melted butter. Cover the bowl with a towel and let the dough rise in a warm place away from drafts for 1 hour, or until it has doubled in size.

While the dough rises, grease heavily a fancy 10-cup mold and then flour it lightly.

When the dough has risen, beat into it the sugar and salt, then pour the dough into the prepared mold; let the dough rise again for 45 minutes, or until its size has doubled.

Bake in a hot 400° oven for 40 minutes, or until the cake is a rich golden brown. Cool the cake in the mold for 5 minutes; turn it out onto a cake rack and cool it completely.

When ready to serve it dribble Almond Glaze, (See p. 176) over the top of the cake, letting it run down the sides. Garnish the top with a wreath of almonds, red and green cherries and golden raisins.

If you prefer not to use saffron, yellow cake coloring may be used.

QUICK ORANGE STREUSEL CAKE

2 cups cake flour, sifted	**1 egg, slightly beaten**
½ cup granulated sugar	**½ cup skim milk**
2 tsp. baking powder	**½ cup orange juice**
¾ tsp. salt	**⅓ cup cooking oil**
1 Tbsp. grated orange rind	

Mix and sift the flour, sugar, baking powder and the salt into a bowl. Stir in the grated rind. Make a well and add the remaining ingredients. Mix only enough to dampen the flour (the batter will be lumpy).

Turn the batter into a greased and floured round 10-inch pan. Sprinkle with Streusel Topping, (See p. 178). Bake in a 375° oven for about 35 minutes.

FLUFFY COFFEE CAKE

1½ cakes quick yeast	**½ stick butter**
1 Tbsp. granulated sugar	**½ cup granulated sugar**
1 cup milk, scalded and cooled	**¼ tsp. salt**
4½ cups all-purpose flour, sifted	**2 eggs, beaten**

Dissolve the yeast and 1 Tbsp. of sugar in the lukewarm milk. Add in 1½ cups of flour. Beat this mix until it is smooth. Cover the bowl with a cloth and let it rise in a warm place until the dough has doubled in size (about 45 minutes).

Cream the butter, then add the sugar and the salt. Add this to the yeast mixture. Add in the eggs and the remaining flour. Knead lightly (see *Glossary*). Place the dough in a greased bowl, cover it with the cloth, and let the dough rise again until it has doubled in size (about 2 hours).

Roll the dough ½ inch thick and place it in 2 well-greased shallow pans, 13 × 9 × 2-inches deep. Let the dough stand and rise again until it has doubled in height.

Prick the top of the dough with a fork, brush with melted butter, and sprinkle on Honey Nut Topping, (See p. 177). Then let the dough rise once again for about an hour. Bake in a 400° oven for 20 minutes. This recipe makes 2 cakes.

BLUEBERRY COFFEE CAKE

3 Tbsp. shortening	1 tsp. salt
½ cup granulated sugar	1 cup milk
1 egg, beaten	¾ cup blueberries, (drained)
2⅔ cups all-purpose flour, sifted	either fresh, canned or frozen (thawed)
3 tsp. baking powder	

Cream the shortening with the sugar. Add the egg (beaten thick and light). Mix and sift the flour (except 3 Tbsp.) with the baking powder and the salt. Add the flour to the first mixture alternately with the milk. Sprinkle the remaining flour over the berries and fold them into the batter quickly.

Bake in a well greased and lightly floured shallow 10-inch square pan for 30 minutes in a 375° oven.

RAISED COFFEE CAKE

1 cup milk, scalded	⅔ cup granulated sugar
1 cake yeast	¾ tsp. salt
¼ cup warm water	4 Tbsp. shortening, melted
2 cups all-purpose flour, sifted (scant)	Sugar and cinnamon (to sprinkle on top)
1 egg, lightly beaten	

Cool the milk. Soften the yeast in the warm water. Add the yeast and 1 cup of the flour into the milk. Beat well and let the mixture rise until it has doubled in size. Then add in the lightly beaten egg. Add the sugar, the salt and the shortening. Mix thoroughly. Add in the remaining flour and mix well. Cover the bowl with a cloth and let the dough rise until the quantity is almost double.

Pour the dough into a shallow well-greased pan, $10 \times 6 \times 2$ inches. Cover this with the cloth and let the dough rise once again. When it has nearly doubled in size, sprinkle the dough thickly with sugar and cinnamon.

Bake for 20 minutes in a hot oven at 400°. Serve the cake while it is hot.

BRUNCH CAKE

1 cake active dry yeast
¼ cup warm water (not hot)
¼ cup granulated sugar
⅝ stick butter, melted
1½ tsp. salt
⅓ cup scalded milk
1 egg, unbeaten

½ tsp. vanilla
2 cups all-purpose flour, sifted
½ cup brown sugar, firmly packed
½ cup flaked, shredded coconut
1 cup pineapple tidbits, drained and cut up

Soften the yeast in the warm water.

Combine in a mixing bowl the sugar, ¼ stick of butter, the salt and the milk (cooled to lukewarm). Stir in the egg; add the vanilla and the softened yeast. Gradually add in the flour, beating well.

Cover the bowl with a cloth and let the dough rise in a warm place (about 85 to 90°) until the dough has doubled in size (for about 45 to 60 minutes).

Meanwhile, melt ⅜ stick of butter (3 Tbsp.) in a 9-inch round deep baking pan. Sprinkle in the brown sugar, the coconut and the pineapple tidbits. Spread the dough into this prepared dish, cover it again and let the dough rise again in a warm place until it has once more doubled in size.

Bake at 350° for 30 to 35 minutes. Remove the cake from the oven, let it cool for about 2 minutes, then invert it onto a rack or plate and sprinkle on some butter crumbled with a little powdered sugar.

BREAKFAST CRUMB CAKE

2 cups all-purpose flour, sifted	⅓ cup granulated sugar
1 tsp. salt	¾ stick butter
¼ tsp. baking soda	1 egg
2½ tsp. baking powder	¾ cup buttermilk

Sift together the flour, salt, soda, baking powder and the sugar. Cut in the butter until the mixture has the consistency of coarse meal.

Beat the egg lightly and add it to the milk; combine this mix quickly with the rest of the batter.

Pour the batter into a buttered and floured 9-inch square cake pan and cover it with Crumb Topping, (See p. 176).

Bake in a hot oven at 400° for 25 to 30 minutes. Makes 8 servings.

RIBBON COFFEE CAKE

2 Tbsp. shortening	2 tsp. baking powder
½ cup granulated sugar	¼ tsp. salt
1 egg, separated and beaten	¼ cup milk
¾ cup all-purpose flour, sifted	½ tsp. vanilla

For Filling

½ cup brown sugar	2 Tbsp. flour
2 tsp. cinnamon	2 Tbsp. melted shortening
1 cup walnut meats, chopped	

Cream the shortening with the sugar; add the beaten egg yolk. Sift the flour with the baking powder and the salt and add it to the egg mix alternately with the milk. Stir in the vanilla. Lastly, fold in the stiffly beaten egg white. Spread one-half of the mixture in a deep, greased and floured 8-inch pie tin.

Mix all the filling ingredients together thoroughly and spread one-half over the batter in the pie tin. Add the rest of the cake batter and top with the second half of the filling.

Bake in a moderate oven, 350–375°, for 45 to 60 minutes. Use the toothpick test to judge when the cake is done.

STRAWBERRY RIPPLE COFFEE CAKE

2 10-oz. pkgs. frozen sliced
strawberries, thawed and
drained
Juice of the strawberries
2 Tbsp. cornstarch
2 cups all-purpose flour, sifted
½ cup granulated sugar
½ tsp. salt

4 Tbsp. baking powder
½ tsp. cinnamon
¼ tsp. mace
1 Tbsp. grated orange rind
1 egg, beaten
1 cup milk
½ stick butter

Combine the strawberry juice and the cornstarch. Cook in a saucepan over moderate heat, stirring constantly until the mix thickens. Cool the mix. Gently stir in the strawberries.

Sift together the flour, sugar, salt, baking powder, and the spices; then stir in the orange rind. Combine the egg, milk and the butter and add them to the dry ingredients, mixing lightly.

Pour the batter into a greased and floured 9-inch square pan. Pour on the strawberry mixture. Bake 375° for 30 to 35 minutes.

QUICK COFFEE CAKE

2 cups all-purpose flour, sifted
¾ tsp. salt
2 tsp. baking powder
½ cup granulated sugar

⅓ cup shortening
1 egg, lightly beaten
¾ cup milk

For Topping

2 Tbsp. flour
½ tsp. cinnamon

¼ stick butter
4 Tbsp. granulated sugar

Sift the flour, salt, baking powder, and the sugar together. With two knives or a pastry blender cut in the shortening. Add the egg combined with the milk. Stir only until all the flour is dampened.

Spread the dough in a greased and floured 8 × 8 × 2-inch pan.

Mix the topping ingredients together and sprinkle them over the dough. Bake in a 400° oven for about 30 minutes.

Spiced and Spicy Cakes
Chapter 4

MOLASSES PEAR CAKE

½ cup boiling water
¼ cup shortening
½ cup molasses
1 egg, beaten
¼ cup granulated sugar
½ tsp. vanilla
1½ cups cake flour, sifted

⅛ tsp. salt
1 tsp. baking soda
¼ tsp. ground cloves
½ tsp. cinnamon
6 pear halves (canned or fresh)
2 Tbsp. chopped nuts
6 maraschino cherries

Pour the boiling water over the shortening and the molasses. Mix the beaten egg, the sugar and the vanilla together thoroughly. Add this mix into the molasses mixture.

Sift together the flour, salt, soda and spices. Add these to the first mixture, beating until all the ingredients are blended.

Pour the batter into a greased and floured 9-inch pie plate, 4 inches deep. Arrange pear halves on top of the cake batter. Sprinkle on the chopped nuts.

Bake in a slow oven at 325° for 45 minutes. When the cake is cool, place a cherry into the hollow of each pear. Serves 5.

RAISIN NUT CAKE

1⅜ sticks butter
1 cup brown sugar
½ cup molasses
2 eggs, beaten
1 tsp. baking soda
1 cup sour milk

2½ cups all-purpose flour,
      sifted
2 tsp. baking powder
½ tsp. cinnamon
½ tsp. ground cloves
1½ cups raisins
½ cup chopped walnuts

Cream the butter with the sugar, then add the molasses, and the eggs. Dissolve the soda in the milk and blend in.

Mix and sift the flour, baking powder, and the spices. Add the raisins and the walnuts to the flour mixture.

Combine the two mixtures and bake in three 9-inch greased and floured layer pans in a 375° oven for 25 minutes.

Cover with a favorite icing.

SOUR CREAM SPICE CAKE

1 stick butter
2 cups brown sugar
3 eggs, separated
2 cups all-purpose flour, sifted
¼ tsp. salt
½ tsp. baking soda

½ tsp. baking powder
1 tsp. ground cloves
½ tsp. allspice
½ tsp. cinnamon
1 cup light sour cream

Cream together the butter and sugar. Add the egg yolks and beat.

Sift together the flour, salt, soda, baking powder and the spices. Add these into the egg yolk mixture, alternately with the sour cream. Now, beat the egg whites stiffly and fold them in.

Bake in a greased and floured 9 × 5-inch loaf pan at 350° for 45 to 50 minutes.

SOFT GINGERBREAD (One-Hundred-Year-Old Recipe)

½ cup shortening
1 cup granulated sugar
1 cup molasses or sorghum
2 eggs
3 cups all-purpose flour, sifted
2 tsp. baking soda
½ tsp. salt

2 tsp. ginger
2 tsp. cinnamon
1 tsp. allspice
½ tsp. ground cloves
½ tsp. nutmeg
1 cup buttermilk

Cream the shortening; add in the sugar gradually; mix thoroughly. Add in the molasses. Beat the eggs well and add them into the creamed mixture.

Sift the flour with the soda, salt, and the spices. Sift a second time. Then add the flour alternately with the buttermilk into the molasses-egg mix. Beat hard to blend the batter thoroughly.

Pour the batter into a greased and floured 9-inch square pan and bake for 45 minutes in a 350° oven.

NUT SPICE CAKE

1 stick butter	1 tsp. baking soda
1 cup brown sugar	½ cup molasses
4 egg yolks	1 cup buttermilk
2½ cups cake flour, sifted	½ cup chopped walnut or
1½ tsp. baking powder	pecan meats
½ tsp. ground cloves	½ cup currants
½ tsp. nutmeg	1 cup chopped raisins
1 tsp. cinnamon	

Cream the butter and the sugar together. Beat the egg yolks and then beat them into the butter blend.

Mix and sift together several times the flour, baking powder, and the spices.

Add the soda and the molasses to the buttermilk.

Then add the sifted flour into the butter-egg mixture, alternately with the buttermilk mix. Lastly, add the nuts and fruits, lightly floured. Mix well.

Bake in a greased and floured 9-inch square pan at 350° for one hour.

GINGER CRUMB CAKE

½ stick butter	½ tsp. salt
½ cup granulated sugar	½ tsp. baking soda
1 egg	1 tsp. cinnamon
½ cup sweet or sour milk	1 tsp. ginger
½ cup molasses	1 cup fine, dry crumbs
¾ cup all-purpose flour, sifted	

Cream the butter and sugar together and beat in the egg.

Mix the milk with the molasses.

Sift the flour, salt and soda and the spices together and add them alternately with the molasses-milk into the creamed butter. Stir in the crumbs. Mix well.

Bake in a greased and floured 8-inch tube pan at 375° for 30 minutes.

SOUR CREAM CAKE

2 eggs, separated	½ tsp. salt
1 cup granulated sugar	½ tsp. nutmeg
1 cup heavy sour cream	½ tsp. cinnamon
1½ cups cake flour, sifted	½ cup chopped nut meats
1 tsp. baking soda	1 cup raisins
1 tsp. baking powder	

Beat the egg yolks; add in the sugar and the sour cream and blend.

Sift the flour, soda, baking powder, salt and spices together and add them to the creamed blend. Add in the nuts and raisins, stirring sparingly.

Beat the egg whites stiffly and fold them into the batter.

Pour the batter into a greased and floured 9 × 5-inch loaf pan. Bake at 350° for 35 to 40 minutes.

MOLASSES GINGER CAKE

¼ cup shortening	¼ tsp. salt
¼ cup granulated sugar	½ tsp. baking soda
1 egg	½ tsp. cinnamon
½ cup molasses	½ tsp. ginger
½ cup hot citrus fruit juice or coffee	¼ tsp. nutmeg
1¼ cups all-purpose flour, sifted	¼ tsp. ground cloves

Cream the shortening with the sugar until they are fluffy and light. Add in the egg and mix well.

Combine the molasses and the hot liquid.

Sift the flour with the salt, soda, and the spices. Add the flour mixture alternately with the molasses liquid into the creamed mixture. Blend thoroughly.

Pour the batter into a greased and floured 8-inch square pan. Bake at 350° for about 35 to 40 minutes.

Cool the cake for several minutes before removing it from the pan. Then slice the cake in half horizontally and fill and frost it with Sea Foam Frosting, (See p. 166).

SPICY PEAR CAKE

⅓ cup shortening
1 egg
¾ cup brown sugar
½ cup raisins
1 cup juice from canned pears
1¾ cups cake flour, sifted

1 tsp. baking soda
¾ tsp. salt
¼ tsp. nutmeg
¼ tsp. ground cloves
½ tsp. cinnamon

Measure the shortening, the egg, and the brown sugar into a large mixing bowl. Dust the raisins lightly with flour and add them in. Then add in the pear juice. Beat with a mixer at medium speed for 1 minute, or 100 vigorous strokes by hand.

Sift the flour, soda, salt and spices together and add them to the first mixture. Mix together at slow speed for one minute, or about 75 strokes by hand.

Pour the batter into an 8-inch greased and floured square pan and bake for 25 to 30 minutes in a 350° oven.

Frost with a favorite icing, or serve with whipped cream.

MOLASSES SPICE CAKE

2 sticks butter
¾ cup brown sugar
¼ cup granulated sugar
4 eggs, separated
½ cup molasses
1 tsp. vanilla
2 cups all-purpose flour, sifted
1 tsp. cinnamon
½ tsp. ground cloves

½ tsp. allspice
½ tsp. mace
¼ tsp. salt
½ tsp. baking powder
½ tsp. baking soda
¾ cup raisins, chopped
1 cup chopped nutmeats
5 Tbsp. milk

Cream the butter. Sift the sugars and add them gradually into the butter. Cream until the mix is smooth.

Beat in the egg yolks; stir in the molasses and the vanilla.

Sift the flour, then resift it with the spices, the salt, the baking powder and baking soda; add these gradually into the batter. Dust a little flour over the raisins and nut meats, then add them into the mixture. Stir in the milk and beat the batter until it is smooth. Finally, beat the egg whites stiffly and fold them in.

Bake in a greased and floured 9-inch tube pan at 350° for about 1 hour.

SPICED BANANA CAKE

⅔ cups shortening	½ tsp. mace
2½ cups cake flour, sifted	¼ tsp. nutmeg
½ tsp. salt	1¼ cups mashed bananas
1⅔ cups granulated sugar	⅔ cup buttermilk
1½ tsp. baking soda	2 large eggs
1½ tsp. cinnamon	⅔ cup chopped nuts

Cream the shortening and sift in the flour, the salt, sugar, soda, and the spices. Add in the bananas and half the buttermilk. Mix until all the flour is dampened. Beat vigorously for 2 minutes. Add in the remaining buttermilk and the eggs. Beat 2 minutes more. Fold in the nuts.

Bake in two greased and floured 8-inch layer cake pans lined with lightly greased wax paper for 30 to 35 minutes. Cool the cakes in the pans on a rack for 5 minutes, then turn them out on the rack and let them cool completely.

Frost with Candy Mountain Frosting (See p. 160), tinted pink. If desired, the frosting can be topped with an additional ½ cup of chopped nuts.

GINGERBREAD

2 sticks butter	2 tsp. baking soda
1 cup granulated sugar	2½ tsp. ginger
4 eggs	¼ tsp. nutmeg
1 cup molasses	¼ tsp. allspice
4 cups all-purpose flour, sifted	1 cup buttermilk
¼ tsp. salt	

Cream the butter with the sugar; add in the eggs, one at a time, beating after each. Stir in the molasses and beat again.

Sift the flour, salt, soda and the spices together. Add these to the molasses mixture alternately with the milk. Beat the batter smooth, then cover it with wax paper and keep it refrigerated until you are ready to use it, or freeze in individual portions for longer storage.

When gingerbread is wanted, pour out the needed quantity into a buttered and floured 8-inch square pan (fill it two-thirds full) and let the batter set until it reaches room temperature. Then bake it in a moderate oven at 325° for about 30 minutes.

This recipe makes 4 or 5 eight-inch square cakes.

Gingerbread can be served either warm or cold, but be sure that it is freshly made. Whipped cream is a delicious topping for gingerbread.

VELVET SPICE CAKE

1½ sticks butter
1½ cups granulated sugar
3 eggs, separated
2 cups cake flour, sifted
1 tsp. baking powder
1 tsp. baking soda
½ tsp. salt
1 tsp. nutmeg
1 tsp. cinnamon
½ tsp. ground cloves
⅞ cup buttermilk

Cream the butter with the sugar; beat in the egg yolks.

Sift together twice the flour, the baking powder, soda, salt and spices. Add them to the creamed mixture alternately with the milk. Beat the egg whites stiffly and fold them in.

Bake in a greased and floured 9-inch tube pan in a 350° oven for 1 hour. Frost with a chocolate or a white icing.

SPICY CHIFFON CAKE

2½ cups cake flour, sifted
1½ cups granulated sugar
1 tsp. salt
3 tsp. baking powder
½ tsp. allspice
½ tsp. cinnamon
½ tsp. nutmeg
¼ tsp. ground cloves
½ cup cooking oil
7 egg yolks, unbeaten
¾ cup cold water
1 cup egg whites (8 large or 10 small eggs)
½ tsp. cream of tartar

Sift the flour, the sugar, the salt, baking powder, and the spices into a mixing bowl. Make a well in this and add the cooking oil, the egg yolks and the water. Beat until the mixture is smooth.

Pour into a large bowl the egg whites and the cream of tartar. Whip until the whites are very stiff. Then pour the egg yolk mixture gradually over the whipped whites, folding in gently. Do not stir.

Pour the batter immediately into an ungreased 10-inch tube pan. Bake at 325° for 55 minutes, then increase the heat to 350° and bake for 10 to 15 minutes longer.

Turn the pan upside down until it is cold, then remove the cake from the pan.

SPICED PRUNE CAKE

1 stick butter	1½ tsp. baking soda
1 cup granulated sugar	½ tsp. cinnamon
2 eggs, well beaten	¼ tsp. ground cloves
1¼ cups chopped cooked prunes	¾ tsp. salt
2 cups all-purpose flour, sifted	½ cup buttermilk

Cream the butter, and add in the sugar. Cream until they are fluffy. Add in the eggs and beat well. Blend in the prunes.

Sift together the flour, soda, spices and salt. Add these into the creamed mixture in three portions, alternately with the buttermilk in two portions. Beat after each addition.

Turn the batter into a greased and floured shallow pan about 12 × 8 inches. Bake at 350° for 35 to 40 minutes.

CHOCOLATE SPICE CAKE

½ cup shortening	2 cups cake flour, sifted
1½ cups granulated sugar	2½ tsp. baking powder
⅔ cup milk	1 tsp. salt
2 squares unsweetened chocolate, melted	½ tsp. cinnamon
4 eggs, separated	¼ tsp. nutmeg
	¾ cup chopped nut meats

Cream the shortening with 1 cup of sugar and 2 Tbsp. of milk until the mix is fluffy. Add in the melted chocolate. Blend thoroughly.

Separate the eggs. Combine the yolks with the remaining milk.

Sift the flour, baking powder, salt and spices together. Add this flour mixture and the mixed milk alternately into the creamed shortening mix, beating well after each addition. Stir in the nuts.

Beat the egg whites stiffly and add in slowly the ½ cup of sugar, beating until the sugar is completely dissolved. Then fold the egg whites into the batter and blend thoroughly.

Pour the batter into two 8-inch greased and floured layer cake pans. Bake for 25 to 30 minutes in a 350° oven.

Frost this cake with a favorite icing, or serve it with whipped cream.

ℜ *Fruit Cakes*
Chapter 5

Note: Many fruit cakes are cooked under steam in many different kinds of containers, but the secret of correctly baking a fruit cake in the oven is this: In the bottom of the oven place your broiler pan filled with boiling water. Keep it filled with boiling water while your cake is baking. You may remove the pan of water during the last fifteen minutes of baking time, and you will find that your cake is perfectly browned, moist and delicious.

AFFLUENT FRUIT CAKE

1 lb. butter
1 lb. granulated sugar
12 eggs, separated
2 tsp. cinnamon
1 tsp. ground cloves
1 tsp. allspice
1 lb. all-purpose flour, sifted
1 (½ pt.) glass plum jelly
5 lbs. white seedless raisins
1 lb. shredded citron

1 lb. candied cherries
1 lb. candied pineapple
1 lb. dates
½ lb. orange peel
½ lb. lemon peel
1 lb. black walnut meats, chopped
½ lb. pecan meats, chopped
1 cup pickled peach juice

Cream the butter and sugar together until they are light and fluffy. Beat the egg yolks well. Sift the spices into one-half of the flour. Beat the egg yolks, the jelly and the spiced flour into the creamed mix. Beat hard for several minutes. Now beat the egg whites stiffly and fold them into the batter.

Cut up all the fruits finely. Dredge them, along with the nuts, in the remaining flour. Then add the floured fruit and nuts into the batter. Mix in the peach juice and stir thoroughly.

This large cake (approximately 12 lbs.) can best be baked in two pans. Divide the batter carefully and pour it into two 10-inch tube pans that have been lined with greased heavy brown paper. Fit the paper into the pans smoothly.

Bake the cakes for 2½ hours in a slow 275° oven.

This cake can be stored for a long time if foil-wrapped, in either an airtight tin or the bottom of the refrigerator.

MOTHER-IN-LAW CAKE

2 cups all-purpose flour, sifted	**½ cup shortening**
½ tsp. salt	**1½ cups granulated sugar**
1 tsp. baking soda	**3 eggs, unbeaten**
½ tsp. baking powder	**1 cup prunes, cooked,**
1½ tsp. cinnamon	**drained, pitted and mashed**
1 tsp. allspice	**1 cup buttermilk**
1 tsp. nutmeg	

Sift together the flour, salt, soda, baking powder, and the spices. Put into another bowl the shortening and sugar and cream them together; add the unbeaten eggs. Beat thoroughly. Now add the prunes to this creamed mixture, and then add the flour mixture alternately with the milk. Blend together.

Pour the batter into two 9-inch layer cake pans that have been well greased and floured. Bake at 350° for about 35 minutes.

Remove the cake from the pans. Allow it to cool. Ice with Caramel Frosting, (p. 161).

TEXAS DARK FRUIT CAKE

1 cup shortening
2 cups brown sugar
8 cups all-purpose flour, sifted
4 tsp. cinnamon
2 tsp. allspice
2 tsp. nutmeg
2 tsp. salt
2 lbs. citron, finely cut
2 lbs. raisins, finely chopped

2 lbs. dates, finely cut
2 lbs. figs, finely cut
2 cups pecan meats, chopped
1 cup walnut meats, chopped
1 cup almonds, chopped
1 cup molasses
2 cups jam (any kind)
4 tsp. baking soda
3 cups buttermilk

Thoroughly cream the shortening with the sugar. Sift four cups of the flour with the spices and the salt. Blend the flour mix in with the shortening and sugar mixture.

Dredge the fruits and the nuts with the other four cups of flour and add them into the mixture. Then add in the molasses and the jam and stir well.

Dissolve the soda in the buttermilk and pour it slowly into the batter; stir continuously while doing so. Mix thoroughly.

Divide the batter into two well greased and lightly floured 10-inch tube pans. Bake at 275° for about three hours. Yield, 2 cakes.

MINCE MEAT FRUIT CAKE

1 (9 oz.) pkg. mince meat
½ cup water
1 cup chopped walnut meats
1 cup (8 oz.) mixed candied
        fruit, chopped
1 (15 oz.) can evaporated
    milk sweetened with 3 tsp.
        granulated sugar

1 egg, beaten
¾ cup all-purpose flour, sifted
½ tsp. baking soda
½ tsp. salt

Break the mince meat into pieces and place it in a 2-quart saucepan. Add in the water and place over heat on top of the stove; stir until all the lumps are broken. Boil briskly for one minute. Remove the pan from the heat and let the mix cool. When the meat has cooled, pour it into a mixing bowl and blend well. Add in the nuts, the candied fruit, the milk, and the egg. Sift the flour with the baking soda and the salt and stir it in until it is just blended.

Grease and flour and then line with wax paper and grease again either a 9-inch tube pan or a 9 × 5 × 3-inch loaf pan. Pour the batter into this. Bake in a moderate oven at 350° for 1 hour and 30 minutes, or until the center of the cake springs back when lightly touched and the top is golden brown. (If a glass baking pan is used reduce the heat to 325°.)

DELICIOUS FRUIT CAKE

¼ lb. mixed orange and lemon peel
¼ lb. citron
1 pkg. pitted dates
½ lb. candied cherries
½ lb. candied pineapple
2½ cups cake flour, sifted
1 small can moist coconut
1 lb. white raisins
1 lb. puffed raisins
2 sticks butter
1 cup granulated sugar

5 eggs
1 tsp. baking powder
1 tsp. salt
1 tsp. cinnamon
½ tsp. nutmeg
½ tsp. ground cloves
½ tsp. allspice
½ cup orange juice
1 (½ pt.) glass cherry or grape jelly
½ lb. whole almonds
½ lb. pecans, chopped

Shred the fruit peel, citron, dates, cherries and pineapple. Then dredge them with ½ cup of flour. Cut the coconut fine and add it in. Add in the raisins.

Cream the butter with the sugar. Add in the eggs and beat. Sift the remaining flour with the baking powder, the salt, and the spices. Then add the spiced flour mix to the creamed mix, alternately with the orange juice and the jelly. Combine in the fruits and the nuts. Mix thoroughly.

Turn the batter into a well-greased 10-inch tube pan lined with wax paper that has been lightly greased. Do not smooth the batter. Garnish the top with a few nuts, candied cherries or grated orange peel.

Bake at 300° for 3½ hours.

FAMOUS FRUIT CAKE

1 cup shortening
1½ cups brown sugar, firmly
            packed
4 eggs
3 cups all-purpose flour, sifted
1 cup thinly sliced citron
1½ cups whole candied
            cherries
1 cup chopped candied
            pineapple

1 cup seedless raisins
1 cup chopped figs
3 cups coarsely chopped nuts
1 tsp. baking powder
2 tsp. salt
2 tsp. cinnamon
2 tsp. allspice
1 tsp. ground cloves
1 cup orange juice

Heat the oven to 275°; line two 9 × 5 × 3-inch greased and floured pans with lightly greased wax paper.

Combine the shortening, the sugar and the eggs. Beat for 2 minutes.

In a large bowl, combine 1 cup of the flour with the fruits and the nuts. Sift the remaining flour with the baking powder, the salt, and the spices. Stir the flour into the shortening mixture alternately with the orange juice. Pour the batter over the fruit mixture; blend well. Turn the batter into the prepared pans.

Bake the cakes for 2½ to 3 hours, or until tested done when a toothpick is inserted. Cool the cakes in the pans on a wire rack. Remove the cakes from the pans; peel off the paper. Wrap the cakes in a cloth dampened in wine or brandy, then cover them tightly with foil and store them for at least one week in a cool place.

Before serving, glaze the top of the cakes (See p. 176) and decorate them with a few nuts and candied fruits. Chill the cakes for easy slicing.

WHITE FRUIT CAKE NO. 1

1 cup shortening
1 cup granulated sugar
5 eggs
2 cups all-purpose flour, sifted
1 tsp. salt
1 tsp. baking soda
1½ tsp. baking powder
¼ cup unsweetened pineapple
            juice
¼ lb. citron, finely cut
¼ lb. candied orange peel,
            finely cut

2 cups almonds, blanched and
            slivered
¼ lb. candied lemon peel,
            finely cut
½ lb. candied cherries, sliced
¼ cup dates, chopped
¼ lb. dried apricots,
            coarsely cut
¼ lb. pressed figs, finely cut
1½ cups pineapple tidbits,
            cut up
¼ lb. moist coconut, shredded
½ lb. white raisins

Thoroughly cream the shortening with the sugar. Add in the eggs, one at a time, beating well after each. Reserve ½ cup of flour for dusting the fruits and nuts. Sift the remaining flour with the salt, the soda, and the baking powder, and add it to the egg mixture alternately with the pineapple juice, beating after each addition.

Dust the fruits, the coconut, and the nut meats with the half cup of flour. Add them in. Stir only until they are blended.

Pour the batter into a well greased and floured 9 × 5 × 3-inch loaf pan, lined with lightly greased wax paper. Decorate the top of the cake with glaced pineapple, almonds, cherries, dates or citron if desired.

Bake at 275° for 1½ hours, then at 300° for 1 more hour.

WHITE FRUIT CAKE NO. 2

2 sticks butter
2 cups granulated sugar
1 cup milk
1 tsp. lemon extract
2 tsp. baking powder
1 tsp. salt
2½ cups cake flour, sifted
1 lb. raisins

1 lb. citron, chopped
½ lb. candied pineapple, cut up
½ lb. candied cherries, cut up
1 lb. almonds, chopped
1 cup coconut, shredded
7 egg whites

Cream the butter and sugar together thoroughly; add the milk and the extract. Sift the baking powder and the salt with the flour and add them in. Dredge the fruits, the almonds, and the coconut in a little flour and blend them in. Lastly, beat the egg whites stiffly and fold them carefully into the batter.

Bake in a greased and floured 10-inch tube pan, lined with lightly greased wax paper, for about 2½ hours at 275°.

GRAHAM FLOUR FRUIT CAKE

1 stick butter
⅔ cup granulated sugar
½ cup molasses
1 cup all-purpose flour, sifted
1 cup graham flour
½ tsp. salt
½ tsp. baking soda
1 tsp. cream of tartar
1 tsp. ground cloves

1 tsp. cinnamon
1 tsp. nutmeg
1 cup raisins
½ cup currants
½ lb. citron, cut fine
½ cup milk
Grated rind of 1 lemon
2 eggs

Cream the butter with the sugar. Add the molasses and blend in.

Sift the flours together. Sift them again with the salt, the soda, cream of tartar, and the spices. Dredge the fruits and citron with a little flour. Add the spiced flour and the fruits to the creamed mixture alternately with the milk. Blend thoroughly, then add in the grated lemon rind. Now beat the eggs slightly and stir them into the batter. Beat the batter thoroughly.

Bake in a foil-lined loaf pan, 9 × 5 × 3-inches, or a foil-lined 9-inch angel food tube pan, in a 275° oven for about 3 hours, or until the cake tests done with the toothpick test.

EASY FRUIT CAKE

1 cup seedless raisins	¾ cup all-purpose flour, sifted
½ stick butter	½ tsp. baking powder
½ cup brown sugar	½ tsp. salt
1 egg	1 lb. candied fruit mix, sliced
1 Tbsp. grated orange rind	

Rinse the raisins in boiling water, then drain them thoroughly.

Cream the butter with the sugar until it is light and fluffy. Beat in the egg and add in the orange peel.

Sift together the flour, baking powder and salt; stir this flour mix into the creamed mixture. Stir together the raisins and the candied fruit and mix then into the batter.

Line a lightly greased 8 × 4 × 2-inch pan with foil. Pour the batter into the pan.

Bake in a slow oven at 275° for about 2 hours. This recipe makes about 2 lbs. of fruit cake.

DATE CAKE

1 (10 oz.) pkg. pitted dates	1 cup chopped nut meats
1 tsp. baking soda	1 tsp. vanilla
1 cup boiling water	1½ cups all-purpose flour, sifted
1 Tbsp. shortening	
1 cup granulated sugar	¼ tsp. salt
1 egg	

Cut the dates into small pieces. Sprinkle on the soda and pour the boiling water over them. Let this mixture cool.

Cream the shortening with the sugar. Add in the egg without separating it. Add in the nuts and the vanilla and beat. Then put in the dates and mix well. Finally, add in the flour and the salt.

Pour the batter into a 9-inch square greased and floured pan and bake at 325° for from 40 to 50 minutes.

CRANBERRY NUT CAKE

2 cups all-purpose flour, sifted
1 cup granulated sugar
1½ tsp. baking powder
½ tsp. baking soda
1 tsp. salt
Juice of one orange and its peel, grated

2 Tbsp. melted shortening
1 egg, well beaten
2 cups fresh cranberries, chopped
1 cup chopped nuts

Sift together the flour, sugar, baking powder, soda and salt.

Combine the orange juice, the grated rind, the melted shortening and enough lukewarm water to make the mixture equal to ¾ cup. Stir this liquid into the dry ingredients and stir in the beaten egg. Fold in the cranberries. Dust the nuts lightly with a little flour and fold them in.

Spoon the mixture into a greased and floured oblong loaf pan 12 × 8 × 2-inches and bake at 350° for 50 to 60 minutes. Let the cake cool and store it in the refrigerator to keep it moist.

PECAN CAKE

1 cup granulated sugar
1 stick butter or margarine
3 eggs
1 cup all-purpose flour, sifted
Pinch of salt
½ tsp. baking powder

½ tsp. cinnamon
½ tsp. nutmeg
2 Tbsp. fruit juice
2 cups raisins
2 cups chopped pecans

Cream the sugar with the shortening. Add the eggs one at a time, stirring well after each.

Sift the flour with the salt, baking powder, and the spices. Add the flour, a little at a time, to the egg mixture, stirring in each addition thoroughly. Add the fruit juice. Flour the raisins and the pecans and stir them into the batter.

Bake in a well-greased and lightly floured 9-inch tube or loaf pan in a 350° oven for about 1 hour, 10 minutes.

Cakes That Top Themselves and Somersault
Chapter 6

PRUNE AND APRICOT UPSIDE DOWN CAKE

½ stick butter
½ cup brown sugar
½ tsp. lemon rind, grated
24 canned apricot halves
        (approx.)
30 cooked prune halves
        (approx.)
5 Tbsp. shortening

⅔ cup granulated sugar
1 egg, beaten
2¼ cups all-purpose flour,
        sifted
4 tsp. baking powder
½ tsp. salt
1 cup milk

Blend the butter with the brown sugar; add in the lemon rind; spread this mixture on the bottom of a cake pan 8 inches square by 2 inches deep. Arrange the apricot and prune halves to form a design on top of the sugar mixture in the pan.

Cream the shortening; add in the white sugar gradually; then add the beaten egg. Beat well. Sift the flour, baking powder, and the salt together and then add them alternately with the milk into the creamed sugar. Mix thoroughly.

Pour the batter carefully over the fruit in the pan. Bake for about 50 minutes at 350°. When done, let the cake cool a few minutes in the pan. Then loosen the sides of the cake with a spatula very gently and invert the cake onto a serving plate. Do this carefully as the fruit serves as the topping. This cake may be served warm, with or without whipped cream.

HANDY ANDY CAKE

2 cups cake flour, sifted	½ cup shortening
3 tsp. baking powder	¾ cup milk
1 tsp. salt	1 tsp. vanilla
1¼ cups granulated sugar	2 eggs

For Topping

2 egg whites	½ cup chopped walnut or
1 cup brown sugar	pecan meats

Sift the flour. Measure it; then sift it again with the baking powder, the salt, and the sugar into a large mixing bowl. Add in the shortening, the milk, and the vanilla. Beat for 2 minutes with an electric mixer at low speed or 150 strokes by hand. Add in the unbeaten eggs. Beat 1 minute longer.

Pour the batter into a 13 × 9 × 2-inch loaf pan which has been greased and floured.

Prepare the topping by beating the egg whites until they are stiff but not dry. Add the brown sugar gradually and beat until it is well combined. Spread this mix on top of the batter. Sprinkle on the nuts.

Bake the cake in a 350° oven for about 35 minutes. Allow the cake to cool before serving it.

TOPSY TURVY CAKE

⅞ stick butter	½ tsp. lemon extract
2 Tbsp. light cream	1½ cups granulated sugar
¾ cup brown sugar, packed	1½ cups cake flour, sifted
¾ cup coconut	1½ tsp. baking powder
¾ cup chopped nuts	½ tsp. salt
3 eggs	¾ cup milk
1 tsp. vanilla	

Prepare the frosting first as follows: Heat 5 Tbsp. of butter ($\frac{5}{8}$ stick) and the cream in a saucepan; stir in the brown sugar, the coconut and the nuts. Cook gently, stirring until everything is well blended. Then spread this mix evenly into an 8 × 12-inch baking pan and set the pan aside while making the cake.

To make the cake: Put the eggs, the vanilla, and the lemon extract into a mixing bowl and beat them lightly with a rotary beater. Add in the white sugar gradually and beat until the mix is fluffy. Sift the flour, the baking powder, and the salt together. Add these to the egg mixture and beat thoroughly. Heat the milk and 2 Tbsp. butter together just to boiling point. Add this gradually into the batter and beat slightly.

Pour the batter over the frosting in the pan and bake at 350° for 35 minutes. When the cake is done invert it on a rack to cool. Any frosting that sticks to the pan can be scraped out while hot and spread on the cake. Serves 12.

RHUBARB UPSIDE DOWN CAKE

1½ cups all-purpose flour, sifted	2 eggs, well beaten
¼ tsp. salt	1 cup granulated sugar
1½ tsp. baking powder	½ cup hot water
	1 tsp. vanilla

For Topping

4 cups sliced rhubarb	¼ stick butter, melted
½ tsp. cinnamon	1 cup granulated sugar

Place the sliced rhubarb in a well greased 9-inch square pan. Sprinkle on the cinnamon, the melted butter and 1 cup of sugar.

Sift the flour with the salt and the baking powder. Beat the eggs well and gradually add to them 1 cup of sugar. Stir in the hot water and the vanilla. Combine the egg mixture with the dry ingredients.

Bake at 350° for about 50 minutes. Remove the cake from the oven. Let it stand a few minutes, then turn it upside down onto a plate. Let it stand a few minutes longer before removing the pan. Serve this cake warm. (*Note:* This recipe requires no shortening.)

MAPLE UPSIDE DOWN CAKE

⅜ stick butter
1 cup maple sugar
4 slices pineapple
3 eggs, separated
1 cup granulated sugar
¼ cup water

½ tsp. vanilla
½ tsp. lemon extract
1 cup cake flour, sifted
¼ tsp. salt
1½ tsp. baking powder

Melt the butter in a heavy 10-inch skillet. Remove the skillet from the heat, spread the maple sugar over the melted butter and cover it with the sliced pineapple.

Beat the egg yolks and add to them the sugar, water, vanilla and lemon extracts. Beat until the mixture is thick and lemon colored. Sift together the flour, the salt and the baking powder and add them into the egg mix. Beat for 3 minutes. Beat the egg whites stiff but not dry and fold them in.

Pour the batter over the pineapple and bake in the skillet at 350° for about 45 minutes. Let the cake cool for a few minutes in the skillet. Then loosen the sides of the cake with a spatula very thoroughly but carefully, in order to keep the bottom intact since it is the topping. Invert the cake on a serving plate. It may be served warm. Serves 8.

ORANGE CAKE

1½ cups granulated sugar
Juice of 1 orange
2 Tbsp. grated orange rind
1 cup raisins
½ cup shortening
2 eggs, beaten

1 tsp. baking soda
¾ cup buttermilk
2 cups all-purpose flour, sifted
1 tsp. vanilla
1 Tbsp. lemon juice

Add one-half cup of sugar to the orange juice. Stir until the sugar is dissolved, then set the dish aside.

Pass the orange rind and raisins three times through a food chopper, or chop by hand very finely.

Cream together the shortening and 1 cup of sugar. Add in the eggs. Dissolve the soda in the buttermilk and add these into the egg mixture. Beat thoroughly into this mixture the raisin-rind mix. Next add in the sifted flour, the vanilla, and the lemon juice. Mix together well.

Turn the batter into a greased and floured 11 × 8-inch pan and bake for about 45 minutes in a 325° oven. Remove the cake from the oven, pour the orange juice over it immediately and let it stand until it is cool.

CHERRY UPSIDE DOWN CAKE

Make the cherry mixture first and set it aside to cool.

Cherry Mixture

1 No. 2 can sour red cherries, drained	**1 cup granulated sugar**
¼ cup juice from the canned cherries	**¼ cup water**
	⅛ stick butter

Boil the cherry juice, the sugar, and the water together until the mixture spins a thread. Add the drained cherries and boil rapidly until the mixture again spins a thread. Melt the butter and pour it into the candied cherries.

Cake Batter

½ stick butter	**¼ tsp. salt**
½ cup granulated sugar	**½ cup milk**
1½ cups all-purpose flour, sifted	**1 egg, well beaten**
2 tsp. baking powder	**1 tsp. vanilla**

Cream the butter and sugar together until they are fluffy. Sift together the flour, the baking powder, and the salt. Mix the flour and creamed mixtures together thoroughly; add in the milk gradually, then the egg and finally add the vanilla.

Pour the candied cherry mixture into a greased and floured 9-inch square pan. Spread the batter over the cherry mixture and bake in a 350° oven for about 45 minutes.

When the cake is removed from the oven, allow it to stand in the pan for 5 minutes. Then loosen the sides of the cake; turn it out carefully upside down onto a serving plate. If the fruit sticks to the pan, lift it off and place it on the cake. Allow the cake to cool and serve it with whipped cream.

APPLE TREAT CAKE

1 cup all-purpose flour, sifted	4 cups tart apples, peeled and sliced
1½ tsp. baking powder	
½ tsp. salt	1 tsp. cinnamon
½ cup granulated sugar	¼ tsp. nutmeg
½ stick butter	3 Tbsp. melted butter
1 egg, beaten	⅓ cup currant jelly
¼ cup milk	1 Tbsp. hot water

Sift together the flour, baking powder, salt and ¼ cup of sugar. Cut in the butter until the mixture resembles coarse cornmeal. Stir in the beaten egg and the milk. Spread the batter in a greased and floured 8-inch square baking dish. Arrange apple slices in parallel rows on top, slightly overlapping each other. Sprinkle on a mixture of the cinnamon, nutmeg, ¼ cup of sugar and the melted butter.

Bake in a hot oven at 400° for 35 minutes, or until the apples are tender.

Beat the jelly with enough of the hot water to make a syrup. Brush this over the warm cake as soon as it is taken from the oven. Serve the cake warm.

SYBIL HANCOCK'S COCONUT CAKE

1½ cups brown sugar	1 tsp. baking powder
1 egg	1 tsp. vanilla
1 tsp. baking soda	¼ stick butter
1 cup heavy sour cream	1 cup shredded coconut
1½ cups cake flour, sifted	

Place 1 cup of the brown sugar in a mixing bowl; add the egg and beat them together.

Dissolve the soda in the sour cream and add this into the sugar mixture. Sift the flour with the baking powder; add it in. Then add in the vanilla. Mix well.

Stir together the butter, the ½ cup of brown sugar and the coconut. Line an 8-inch square pan with this mix. Pour the batter over it.

Bake in a 325° oven for 35 to 40 minutes. Remove the pan from the oven and when the cake is cool to the touch, turn the cake upside down on a serving plate. The coconut becomes the topping.

DATE CRUMB CAKE

2 cups all-purpose flour, sifted	1 cup buttermilk
1 cup granulated sugar	2 eggs, beaten
1¼ sticks butter	1 cup (5 oz.) dates, chopped
⅓ cup brown sugar	½ cup nut meats, chopped
1 tsp. baking soda	1 tsp. vanilla

Mix the flour, sugar and the butter together until the mixture resembles coarse meal. Set aside one cup of this mixture and add the brown sugar to it. This is the topping.

Dissolve the soda in the buttermilk. Add this and the eggs to the remaining mixture. Mix well. Then add the dates and the nuts. Finally, add the vanilla.

Pour the batter into a greased and floured 13 × 9 × 2-inch pan. Cover it with the topping. Bake at 375° for about 30 to 35 minutes.

DUTCH APPLE BRAN CAKE

1½ cups all-purpose flour, sifted	½ cup shortening, softened
2 tsp. baking powder	½ cup granulated sugar
½ tsp. salt	1 egg
½ cup whole bran cereal	½ cup milk

Sift together the flour, baking powder and salt. Mix this in with the bran cereal.

Blend the shortening with the sugar; add the egg. Beat well. Add the sifted flour mix into the egg-sugar mixture alternately with the milk, mixing after each addition.

Place the batter in a greased and floured 9-inch square pan. Then prepare the topping as follows:

Topping

3 cups sliced, pared tart apples	2 tsp. cinnamon
½ cup brown sugar, (packed)	¼ stick butter

Arrange the apples on top of the batter. Combine the sugar and the cinnamon and sprinkle them over the apples. Dot the butter on top.

Bake the cake in a moderate oven at 375° for about 30 minutes.

QUICK ORANGE CAKE

1 stick butter, melted and hot	¼ tsp. salt
1 cup granulated sugar	¾ cup orange juice
2 eggs	Grated rind of 2 oranges
2 cups all-purpose flour, sifted	3 Tbsp. granulated sugar
4 tsp. baking powder	

Add the hot butter to 1 cup of sugar and beat thoroughly. Add the eggs one at a time, beating after each addition. Sift the flour, baking powder, and the salt together, and add them alternately with the orange juice to the first mixture. Blend in well; beat again.

Pour the batter into a greased and floured 8-inch square pan. Mix the orange rind with the 3 Tbsp. sugar and sprinkle on top. Bake for 50 minutes at 350°.

CHOCOLATE TOPSIDE CAKE

¼ stick butter, melted	2 tsp. baking powder
¾ cup granulated sugar	½ cup milk
1 cup cake flour, sifted	1 tsp. vanilla
Pinch of salt	¼ cup nut meats, chopped
2 Tbsp. cocoa	

For Topping

2 Tbsp. cocoa	½ cup granulated sugar
½ cup brown sugar	1 cup cold water

To make the batter, cream the butter and the sugar in a mixing bowl. Sift together the flour, salt, cocoa, and the baking powder. Add these to the first mixture. Blend well. Stir in the milk and the vanilla. Blend thoroughly. Add the nuts, then stir again. Pour the batter into a greased and floured 9-inch square heatproof glass pan.

Mix together the four topping ingredients and pour the mixture over the batter.

Bake for 40 minutes in a moderate 350° oven for 35 to 40 minutes. Serve this cake directly from the pan.

FRUIT SALAD CAKE (without Shortening)

1½ cups cake flour, sifted
½ tsp. salt
1 cup granulated sugar
1 tsp. baking soda
1 tsp. baking powder

2 cups cooked mixed fruit or berries, including about ¾ cup light syrup
1 egg
1 tsp. vanilla

For Topping

1 cup brown sugar
1 Tbsp. all-purpose flour

1 cup chopped nuts

Sift together the flour, salt, sugar, soda and baking powder. Add in the fruit and juice to these dry ingredients. Combine well.

Beat the egg and add it into the mixture. Lastly, stir in the vanilla. Mix well.

Pour the batter into a greased and floured 9-inch square pan.

Mix the brown sugar and the Tbsp. of flour together for the topping and sprinkle them over the batter in the pan. Finally, cover with the nuts.

Bake at 325° for about 55 minutes.

APPLESAUCE CAKE NO. 1 (Eggless)

½ cup shortening
1 cup granulated sugar
1 cup applesauce
1 cup raisins, chopped
2½ cups all-purpose flour, sifted

½ tsp. ground cloves
½ tsp. nutmeg
½ tsp. cinnamon
1 tsp. baking soda
½ tsp. salt

For Topping

2 Tbsp. brown sugar

1 tsp. cinnamon

Cream the shortening and the sugar together; add in the applesauce. Combine well.

Mix the raisins with ½ cup of the flour. Sift the remaining flour with the spices, the soda, and the salt, and add these dry ingredients into the liquid mixture. Beat well.

Pour the batter into a greased and floured 9-inch tube pan. Cover with the combined topping ingredients. (Sprinkle all over.) Bake at 300° to 325° for about 1 hour.

BANANA TEA CAKE

¼ cup shortening
¼ cup granulated sugar
1 egg, beaten
4 tsp. baking powder

¼ tsp. salt
2 cups cake flour, sifted
1 cup milk
1½ cups mashed bananas

For Topping

½ cup granulated sugar
blended with 2 tsp. cinnamon

Blend the sugar with the shortening and the beaten egg.

Sift the baking powder, salt and flour together. Add the flour to the first mixture, alternately with the milk. Mix the batter together well. Then fold in the bananas.

Pour the batter into a greased and floured 9-inch square pan. Sprinkle on the topping and bake for 30 minutes in a 400° oven.

FRESH APPLE CAKE

1 cup granulated sugar
½ cup shortening
2 eggs, beaten
1 cup tart apples, ground or
                    grated
2 cups all-purpose flour, sifted
1 tsp. baking soda

½ tsp. salt
1 cup chopped pecan meats
1½ Tbsp. buttermilk
1 tsp. vanilla
3 Tbsp. granulated sugar
1 tsp. cinnamon

Cream 1 cup of sugar with the shortening. Add in the eggs and the apples. Mix well.

Sift the flour with the soda and the salt and add in the nuts. Mix the floured nuts into the egg-apple mix. Stir in the buttermilk and the vanilla. Combine well.

Pour the batter into a greased and floured 10 × 6 × 3-inch loaf pan. Sprinkle the top with a mixture of the 3 Tbsp. of sugar and the 1 tsp. of cinnamon. Bake for 1 hour in a 350° oven.

GRAPE UPSIDE DOWN CAKE

2 lbs. Concord grapes	1⅓ cups granulated sugar
¾ cup granulated sugar	½ cup shortening
2¼ cups cake flour, sifted	1 cup milk
2½ tsp. baking powder	2 eggs
1 tsp. salt	1 tsp. vanilla

Wash the grapes. Separate the skins from the pulp and save them. Cook the pulp until it is soft; sieve to remove the seeds. Add in the skins, stir in the ¾ cup of sugar and cook until the skins are tender (about 15 minutes). This makes about 2 cups of pulp.

Sift the flour, baking powder, salt, and the remaining 1⅓ cups of sugar together into a mixing bowl. Add in the shortening, ½ cup of milk, the eggs, and the vanilla. Beat for 2 minutes. Add the remaining milk; beat for 30 seconds.

Pour the batter into a well-greased and lightly floured 9 × 13-inch pan. Spread the grape pulp over it. Bake in a moderate oven at 350° for about 45 minutes. Serve the cake warm, with whipped cream. *Note:* The grape layer sinks to the bottom while the cake is baking and makes an upside down cake. Therefore turn the cake out upside down before serving it.

℘ Budget-Minded Cakes
Chapter 7

KANSAS SUNFLOWER CAKE

½ cup shortening	1 cup granulated sugar
2 cups cake flour, sifted	3 egg yolks
2½ tsp. baking powder	¾ cup milk
¼ tsp. salt	1 tsp. vanilla

Place the shortening in a mixing bowl; let it soften. Sift the flour, the baking powder, the salt, and the sugar together into a bowl. Add in the remaining ingredients, including the shortening. Beat vigorously until the batter is smooth.

Bake in 2 greased and floured 8-inch layer cake pans lined with lightly greased wax paper for 20 to 30 minutes in a preheated 350° oven.

Frost as desired.

(*Note:* This gold cake might be made at the same time Featherweight Cake No. 2 is made—to use up the leftover egg whites.)

ECONOMY CAKE

2 cups brown sugar	1 Tbsp. cold water
½ cup shortening	2½ cups cake flour, sifted
2½ Tbsp. cocoa	1 cup sour milk
½ cup hot water	1 tsp. vanilla
1 tsp. baking soda	

Cream together the sugar and the shortening.

Dissolve the cocoa in the hot water and add it to the creamed mixture. Blend thoroughly. Dissolve the soda in the cold water and add it to the mixture.

Then sift in the flour, adding it in alternately with the sour milk. Finally, add in the vanilla. Beat the batter until it is smooth.

Bake in a greased and floured 9-inch square pan at 350° for 40 to 45 minutes.

Ice with either a white or a chocolate icing.

SUNDAY SUPPER CAKE

1½ cups cake flour, sifted
1½ tsp. baking powder
¼ tsp. salt
1 cup granulated sugar
½ stick butter
2 eggs

½ cup milk
1 tsp. flavoring extract
1 (4 oz.) bar sweet chocolate, grated
½ cup chopped nut meats

Sift together the flour, the baking powder, and the salt.

Cream the sugar with the butter, then add the unbeaten eggs and blend well together. Add in the sifted dry ingredients alternately with the milk. Add the flavoring. Beat this batter for 2 or 3 minutes with a rotary beater or an electric mixer until it is light and very smooth.

Pour the batter into a greased and floured 8-inch square pan. Mix together the grated chocolate and the nuts and cover the batter evenly with them. Bake in a moderate oven at 350° for 35 to 40 minutes.

SUGARLESS ORANGE CAKE

2¼ cups cake flour, sifted
2¼ tsp. baking powder
¼ tsp. salt
½ cup shortening

2 tsp. grated orange rind
1 cup light corn syrup
2 eggs
½ cup orange juice

Sift the flour before measuring it, then sift it three times with the baking powder and the salt.

Cream the shortening with the orange rind. Add in the syrup very gradually, a tablespoonful at a time, beating hard after each addition to keep the mixture thick. Add in about one-fourth of the flour. Beat again until the mixture is smooth. Add the unbeaten eggs, one at a time, beating well after each. Then add in the remaining flour in thirds, alternating with the orange juice, and beat well after each addition.

Bake in two greased and floured 8-inch layer pans in a moderate oven at 375° for 30 minutes, or in a 9-inch square loaf pan for 40 minutes.

Top with Sugarless Orange Frosting, (See p. 168).

MRS. ALICE PEET'S EGGLESS CAKE

½ cup shortening	⅛ tsp. salt
1 cup granulated sugar	1 tsp. baking soda
1½ cups all-purpose flour, sifted	1 cup buttermilk
⅓ cup cocoa	1 tsp. vanilla

Cream the shortening and the sugar together carefully. Sift the flour, cocoa, salt and soda together about three times, then add them to the creamed mixture alternately with the buttermilk. Stir in the vanilla.

Bake in two 8-inch greased and floured layer cake pans at 325° for 25 to 30 minutes. Remove the layers from the pans and let them cool. Then put them together with Uncooked Icing, (See p. 175), and dot the top with chocolate chips.

PIN MONEY CAKE

1 cup granulated sugar	1 egg, well beaten
½ stick butter	½ tsp. baking soda
1¾ cups cake flour, sifted	1 cup buttermilk
½ tsp. baking powder	½ tsp. lemon extract

Cream together thoroughly the sugar and the butter. Sift the flour with the baking powder and add it to the creamed mixture. Add in the egg and stir.

Dissolve the soda in the buttermilk and pour it gradually into the first mixture. Add the lemon extract and beat the whole batter vigorously.

Bake in an 8-inch greased and floured tube pan in a 375° oven for 35 to 40 minutes.

Frost with Carrot Frosting, (See p. 161).

TWO EGG CAKE

2 cups cake flour, sifted
2½ tsp. baking powder
¾ cup granulated sugar
½ tsp. salt
½ cup shortening

¾ cup white corn syrup
½ cup milk
2 eggs, unbeaten
1½ tsp. vanilla

Sift the flour, the baking powder, the sugar, and the salt into a mixing bowl. Drop in the shortening, then pour in the corn syrup and ¼ cup of milk. Beat with a mixing spoon 150 strokes or for 1 minute. Add in the eggs and beat 250 strokes, or for almost 2 minutes. Add the remaining ¼ cup of milk and the vanilla. Beat 50 strokes, or for 20 seconds. Scrape the bowl and spoon often during the beatings.

Pour the batter into two 8-inch greased and floured layer cake pans lined with lightly greased wax paper. Bake in a 375° oven for 25 to 35 minutes, or until the cake tests done with a toothpick.

Cool the cake in the pans for 10 to 15 minutes on a wire rack before carefully removing it from the pans and taking off the paper.

Ice with Snow Peak Icing, (See p. 175).

EGGLESS CHOCOLATE CAKE

1½ cups all-purpose flour,
                    sifted
¾ cup granulated sugar
¼ tsp. salt
1 tsp. baking soda

¼ stick butter
1½ squares unsweetened
            chocolate, melted
1 cup milk
¼ tsp. vanilla

Sift together the flour, sugar, salt and soda. Cream the butter with the melted chocolate. Stir these two mixes into one batter. Add in the milk and the vanilla, then beat thoroughly.

Bake in one 9-inch greased and floured layer cake pan in a moderate 350° oven for 25 to 30 minutes, or until the cake springs back from a light touch and shrinks slightly from the side of the pan. Turn it out on a cake rack and let it cool.

When the cake is cold, cut it horizontally in half. Put the two slices together with a boiled white icing or Chocolate Icing, (See p. 171).

EGGLESS, MILKLESS, BUTTERLESS CAKE

2 cups brown sugar	½ tsp. ground cloves
2 cups hot water	½ tsp. cinnamon
4 Tbsp. shortening	2 tsp. baking soda
1½ cups seedless raisins	1 Tbsp. lukewarm water
1 tsp. salt	3 cups all-purpose flour, sifted

Put into a saucepan the brown sugar, the hot water, the shortening, the raisins, the salt, and the spices. Boil these together for 5 minutes, stirring occasionally. Pour this mix into a mixing bowl and allow it to cool.

When the mixture is cold, dissolve the soda in the lukewarm water and add it in. Sift in the flour gradually, stirring and blending thoroughly.

Pour the batter into two small 8 × 4-inch greased and floured loaf pans and bake at 300° for 1¼ hours. Frost the cakes with Quick Caramel Frosting, (See p. 166).

BREAD CRUMB CAKE (No Shortening Required)

3 eggs	¼ tsp. cinnamon
1 cup granulated sugar	¼ tsp. salt
2 cups rolled crumbs from very dry toast	½ tsp. almond extract
	1 tsp. vanilla

Beat the eggs; add in the sugar; stir in the remaining ingredients. Combine well.

Pat the mixture evenly into a shallow 11 × 7-inch greased and floured loaf pan. Bake in a very moderate oven at 300° for about 30 minutes.

Ice to taste, or serve with whipped cream.

Eggs are the only leavening in the cake, giving it somewhat the texture and flavor of macaroons. (This is an excellent way to use up stale bread.)

❧ Baked in the Refrigerator
Chapter 8

RASPBERRY LOAF CAKE

1 pkg. (1 lb.) frozen raspberries, thawed

⅓ cup raspberry juice (from
package)

1 (8 oz.) pkg. cream cheese,
softened

1 (12 oz.) loaf pound cake

For Sauce

¾ cup raspberry juice
2 Tbsp. cornstarch

1 cup light sour cream

Drain the raspberries, reserving the liquid. Beat the cream cheese until
it is fluffy and gradually add in the raspberry juice.

Slice the pound cake horizontally into 4 equal layers. On each of
3 layers spread 2 Tbsp. of the cream cheese mixture and top with one-third
of the raspberries. Stack the layers, ending with the plain fourth layer.
Chill the cake in the refrigerator until it has set. Also refrigerate the
remaining cream cheese mixture (but do not let it stiffen).

After the cake has set, frost its top and sides with the reserved cream
cheese mixture. Then chill the cake for several hours. Meanwhile prepare
the raspberry sauce, as follows.

Combine the raspberry juice and the cornstarch in a small saucepan. Cook on top of stove over medium heat, stirring constantly until the mixture thickens and loses its cloudy quality. Remove the pan from the heat and allow the mixture to cool. Then gently fold it into the sour cream.

Serve slices of loaf topped with raspberry sauce. This recipe will serve 8.

Note: If the frozen raspberries do not yield enough juice, add some diluted raspberry sauce from the bottled variety that can be found in most grocery stores.

CHRISTMAS DAY CAKE

4 cups milk	¾ cup granulated sugar
2 envelopes unflavored gelatin	1 tsp. vanilla
2 egg yolks	2 egg whites, stiffly beaten
¼ tsp. salt	1½ cups heavy cream, whipped
¾ cup chopped maraschino cherries	1 12-oz. pkg. vanilla wafers
⅓ cup cherry juice	

Place 1 cup of milk in a small bowl and sprinkle in the gelatin. Allow it to soften.

In a double boiler, scald 3 cups of milk. Meanwhile beat the egg yolks with a fork. Pour the salt into the egg yolks, add them to the scalded milk and cook, stirring until the mixture coats a spoon. Allow the mixture to cool a few minutes; then add the cherries, the cherry juice, the sugar, and the vanilla extract. Stir until the sugar is dissolved.

Now refrigerate the mixture, stirring it occasionally, until it is completely cold and begins to thicken. Then fold in the beaten egg whites and half of the whipped cream.

Lightly butter a 9-inch spring form pan. Line the bottom and sides of the pan with vanilla wafers, pour in the filling and arrange more vanilla wafers on top. Refrigerate the cake for at least 12 hours.

At serving time, unmold the cake and frost it with the rest of the whipped cream.

UPSIDE DOWN ICE CREAM CAKE

1 can (1 lb. 14 oz.) fruit cocktail	1 baked round cake layer (white or gold, 8 or 9 inches in diameter)
1 quart vanilla or strawberry ice cream	

Drain the fruit cocktail well. Spread the fruit in an 8 or 9-inch round pan. Spoon the ice cream over the fruit. Top with the cake layer.
Wrap the pan in foil and freeze it in the refrigerator.
To serve, take off the foil and dip the pan in warm water until the cake can be loosened. Turn out upside down onto a serving plate. Makes 6 to 9 portions.

APRICOT-PINEAPPLE CHEESE CAKE

½ cup crushed pineapple, well drained (save the juice)	¼ cup apricot juice
1½ cups canned apricot halves, well drained (save the juice)	1 pkg. lemon flavored gelatin
	¼ cup granulated sugar
	1 cup heavy cream, whipped
1¼ tsp. salt	½ cup finely crushed graham cracker crumbs
2 cups dry cottage cheese, lightly packed and sieved	¼ stick butter, melted
¼ cup pineapple juice	3 Tbsp. finely chopped nuts

Place the pineapple in a medium size mixing bowl. Press the apricots through a sieve (there should be one cup of apricot pulp) and combine them with the pineapple. Add in the salt and cheese and blend thoroughly.
Bring the apricot and pineapple juices to a boil and dissolve the gelatin in them. Allow this liquid to cool slightly. Gradually add ⅔ cup of the cheese mixture to the gelatin mixture. Combine with the remaining cheese mixture. Blend thoroughly.
Blend the sugar lightly into the whipped cream. Carefully fold this into the cheese mixture.
Pile the batter lightly into a well greased 8-inch spring form pan. Chill the pan in the refrigerator for several hours or overnight. Unmold the cake onto a plate. Combine the crumbs with the butter and add

in the nuts. Sprinkle this blend over the top and sides of the chilled cheese cake. Serves 8.

UNBAKED FRUIT CAKE

1 lb. graham crackers
1 lb. dates, cut fine
1 lb. golden raisins
1 cup English walnuts,
cut fine

1 lb. marshmallows, cut into
bits
1 lb. red and green gumdrops,
cut into bits
½ cup granulated sugar
1 cup heavy cream, whipped

Crush the crackers into crumbs. Mix in the chopped fruits, the nuts, the marshmallows and the gumdrops. Add in the sugar and the whipped cream, blending well.

Pack the mixture very tightly into two 9 × 5-inch loaf pans and wrap them snugly with aluminum foil. Let the pans stand in the refrigerator for about two weeks before using the cakes.

REFRIGERATOR FRUIT CAKE

1½ cups seedless raisins
1 cup prunes
1 cup pitted dates, cut up
1½ cups mixed candied fruits
and peels, cut finely
1   stick butter or margarine
½ cup confectioners sugar
¼ cup light corn syrup

½ cup marmalade
1 tsp. cinnamon
1 tsp. ground cloves
½ tsp. salt
½ cup walnut meats, chopped
5 cups finely crushed graham
cracker crumbs

Wash and drain the raisins. Pour boiling water over the prunes and let them stand for 5 minutes. Then drain, cool, slice and pit them. Combine all the fruits and peels.

Cream the butter with the sugar; blend in the syrup, the marmalade, spices, and the salt. Mix this in with the fruit; let it stand for 2 hours. Then blend in the walnuts and the crumbs.

Pack the mixture into a 9 × 5 × 3-inch loaf pan, which has been lined with wax paper. Chill the cake in the refrigerator for 48 hours or longer.

QUICK CHEESE CAKE

1¼ cups graham cracker crumbs

1 stick butter or margarine, melted

1 (8 oz.) pkg. cream cheese

2 cups milk

1 (3¾ oz.) pkg. Pineapple Cream Instant Pudding powder

Make a graham cracker crust by combining the butter with the crumbs and pressing them firmly into the bottom of a 9-inch round layer cake pan. Set this in the refrigerator to chill until needed.

Stir the cream cheese until it is very soft. Gradually blend in ½ cup of milk until the mix is smooth and creamy. Add in the remaining milk and the pudding powder slowly. Beat slowly with an egg beater for 1 minute. (Do not overbeat). Pour this mixture onto the cooled cracker crust. Sprinkle some extra graham cracker crumbs over the top of the cake to make it extra crunchy. Then chill the cake in the refrigerator.

(To make Lemon Cheese Cake, use Lemon Instant Pudding powder instead of the Pineapple Cream.)

LEMONADE CHEESE CAKE

3 envelopes unflavored gelatin

1 cup milk

2 eggs, separated

3 cups (24 oz.) creamed cottage cheese

1 (6 oz.) can frozen lemonade concentrate, unthawed

¼ cup granulated sugar

1 cup heavy cream, whipped

For Crust

1½ cups graham cracker crumbs

3 Tbsp. confectioners sugar, sifted

¾ stick butter or margarine, melted

To make the crust, combine the crumbs, butter and confectioners sugar. Reserve ¼ cup for topping. Press the mixture firmly into the bottom of an 8 or 9-inch spring form pan and place it in the refrigerator to chill until needed.

Sprinkle the gelatin on the milk in a 2½-quart saucepan. Add in the egg yolks; stir well. Place the pan on top of the stove over low heat; stir constantly until the gelatin dissolves and the mixture thickens slightly (2 or 3 minutes). Then remove the pan from the heat.

Sieve or beat the cottage cheese in the small bowl of an electric mixer at high speed for 3 or 4 minutes, or by hand with a rotary beater for about 4 minutes, vigorously. Stir the cottage cheese and the lemonade concentrate into the gelatin mixture. Wash the bowl and beaters (fat left on the beater will prevent egg whites from whipping).

Beat the egg whites until they are stiff. Gradually add the sugar and continue beating until the mixture is very stiff. Fold in the gelatin-cheese mix; then fold in the whipped cream.

Pour the cheese mix over the crust and top with the reserved crumbs. Chill the cake in the pan in the refrigerator for about 2 hours. Remove the rim of the spring form and slide the cake (still on the bottom of the pan) onto a serving plate. Makes 8 or 9 servings.

MARMALADE REFRIGERATOR CAKE

2 small pkgs. gingersnaps	3 eggs, separated
1 Tbsp. gelatin	¼ cup orange marmalade
2 Tbsp. cold water	½ cup heavy cream
1 stick salt-free butter	1 tsp. marmalade
¾ cup confectioners sugar	

Line a 7-inch spring form mold with the gingersnaps; crumble bits to fill the bottom completely.

Soften the gelatin in the cold water in a small pan and dissolve it by placing the pan in a bowl of hot water.

Cream the butter with ½ cup confectioners sugar until it is fluffy. Beat the egg yolks well and add them in. Fold in the liquid gelatin and the marmalade.

Beat the egg whites until they are fluffy; gradually add the remaining ¼ cup of sugar to the whites and beat until the mix is ropey (of a meringue-like consistency). Fold the egg whites into the first mixture. Pour the total mixture on top of the gingersnaps.

Chill the mold in the refrigerator for 24 hours. Remove the outer rim but not the base of the mold. Place the cake on the base onto a plate. Decorate the cake with the cream whipped with the 1 tsp. of marmalade and ring with half circles of gingersnaps.

PINEAPPLE DELIGHT CAKE

1 cup crushed pineapple	4 egg yolks, well beaten
½ cup pineapple juice	1 cup chopped pecan meats
1 pkg. lemon gelatin	4 egg whites
1½ cups granulated sugar	¾ lb. vanilla wafers
2 sticks butter	

Drain the crushed pineapple. Heat the pineapple juice to boiling point. Add in the gelatin and stir until it is dissolved. Set this aside to cool.

Cream the sugar with the butter; add in the egg yolks. Then add the pineapple, the gelatin mix and the nuts. Beat the egg whites until they are stiff and fold them into the creamed mixture. Crush the vanilla wafers. Put half the crumbs in a shallow pan about 11 × 7 inches. Pour on the fruit mixture. Spread the rest of the crumbs on top and pat down gently.

Refrigerate the cake for 24 hours.

CHOCOLATE REFRIGERATOR CAKE

¼ lb. sweet chocolate	¼ cup chopped walnuts
1 Tbsp. water	1 egg white, stiffly beaten
1 egg yolk	½ cup heavy cream
1 Tbsp. confectioners sugar	20 vanilla wafers, or 12 lady fingers

Melt the chocolate in a double boiler. Add the water and blend well. Remove the pan from the flame; add in the egg yolk. Beat vigorously. Add the sugar and walnuts. Blend. Fold in the egg white. Whip the cream until it is stiff and forms a peak and then fold it into the chocolate mixture.

Line a shallow refrigerator tray with one-half the vanilla wafers or lady fingers. Pour on the chocolate mixture. Cover with the remaining wafers. Chill the tray in the refrigerator for about 12 hours. Serves 6.

PINEAPPLE WHIPPED CHEESE CAKE

1½ cups fine graham cracker crumbs	1 (9 oz.) can crushed pineapple
¾ stick melted butter or margarine	1 pkg. lemon gelatin
3 Tbsp. confectioners sugar, sifted	2 (8 oz.) pkgs. cream cheese
	¼ cup dry milk powder

Mix the crumbs with the butter and the sugar and press them firmly to line the bottom of a 9-inch square pan. Chill the pan in the refrigerator until it is needed.

Drain the pineapple; save the syrup. Mix the gelatin as directed on the package, using the pineapple syrup as part of the liquid. Do not chill it.

With an electric mixer at low speed, or with a rotary hand beater, gradually beat the gelatin mixture into the cream cheese in a large bowl. Chill the bowl in the refrigerator until the cheese mixture is very thick but not set.

With the mixer at high speed, or rapidly by hand, beat the dry milk powder into the cheese mixture. Keep beating until the cheese lumps disappear and the mixture doubles in volume. Then fold in the drained pineapple. Pour the total mixture over the crumbs in the chilled pan. Chill the pan in the refrigerator until the cake is firm (about 2 hours).

This recipe makes 8 or 9 servings.

VELVETY ICEBOX CAKE

1 Tbsp. gelatin	2 eggs
3 Tbsp. cold water	¾ cup orange juice
1 cup condensed milk	1 tsp. grated orange rind
1 cup water	2 dozen lady fingers or 1
2 Tbsp. cornstarch	medium sponge cake
1 cup granulated sugar	⅔ cup condensed milk
	(chilled for whipping)

Soften the gelatin in the cold water. Dilute the condensed milk with the cup of water. Scald 1¾ cups of this dilution in a double boiler. Mix the cornstarch with the sugar and add it to the scalded milk. Cook for 10 minutes, stirring constantly. Beat the eggs lightly and combine them with the remaining ¼ cup of diluted milk. Add this into the cornstarch mix. Cook a few minutes longer, stirring constantly. Remove the pan from the heat; stir in the softened gelatin. Add the orange juice and grated rind.

Line an 8-inch spring form pan with lady fingers or ½-inch fingers of sponge cake. Fill up the pan with alternate layers of the cooked mixture and fingers. Arrange fingers on top. Chill the cake for 3 or 4 hours in the refrigerator. Serve with the whipped condensed milk. (Condensed milk whips readily if very cold. Also chill the bowl in which it is whipped).

Garnish with cherries or sliced oranges. Serves 8 to 10.

CRANBERRY ORANGE CHEESE CAKE

2 Tbsp. unflavored gelatin	1 tsp. grated lemon rind
½ cup orange juice	1 tsp. lemon juice
2 eggs, separated	3 cups creamed cottage cheese, sieved
½ cup milk	
1 cup granulated sugar	1 cup heavy cream, whipped
½ tsp. salt	2 cups sweetened, cooked whole cranberries
2 Tbsp. grated orange rind	

For Crust

2½ cups graham cracker (or other favorite crumbs)	1⅛ sticks butter or margarine

Combine the crumbs and butter and press them firmly into the bottom of a 13 × 9-inch pan. Chill in the refrigerator until needed.

Soften the gelatin in the orange juice; put this aside.

Beat the egg yolks lightly in a saucepan. Add in the milk, ¾ cup of sugar, and the salt. Cook on top of the stove over low heat, stirring constantly until the mixture thickens. Add in the softened gelatin and stir until it has dissolved. Add in the orange rind, lemon rind, lemon juice, and the sieved cheese. Chill the mixture in the refrigerator until it is partially set.

Then fold in the whipped cream and the cranberries. Lastly, beat the egg whites until they are stiff but not dry and gradually add the remaining ¼ cup of sugar to them. Fold the egg whites into the cheese mixture.

Pour the mixture onto the crust in the pan and chill it in the refrigerator until it is completely set (about 3 hours).

MYSTERY FRUIT CAKE

1 pkg. honey spice cake mix	1½ cups seedless raisins
4 cups candied mixed fruit, cut up	1 cup dates, cut fine
	4½ cups pecans, chopped
½ cup red cherries, cut up	1 pkg. fluffy white frosting mix
½ cup green cherries, cut up	

Make the honey spice cake as directed on the package. Cool the cake and crumble it into a very large bowl. Add the mixed fruit, cherries, raisins, dates, and the nuts.

Prepare the fluffy white frosting as directed on the package, and mix it with the cake and the fruit.

Pack the mixture tightly into a foil-lined loaf pan, 9 × 5 × 2¾ inches. Or in an angel food tube pan. Cover the pan with foil and chill it in the refrigerator for at least 24 hours. Keep the cake refrigerated. To serve cut slices about ¼ inch thick.

CHOCOLATE WHIPPED CREAM CAKE

1 (4 oz.) bar German's sweet chocolate	1 tsp. unflavored gelatin
1 large pkg. (5 oz.) vanilla pudding mix	2 cups milk
	2 cups heavy cream, whipped
2 tsp. instant coffee	15 lady fingers, split

Break the chocolate into squares; set it aside. Combine the pudding mix powder, the coffee and the gelatin in a saucepan. Stir in the milk. Bring to a boil over medium heat, stirring constantly. Remove the pan from heat, add in the chocolate and stir until the mixture is smooth. Cool the mixture completely; then beat it until it is very smooth. Stir in 1½ cups of whipped cream.

Line an 8 × 4 × 3-inch loaf pan with wax paper. Let the paper extend beyond the pan's rim. Line the bottom and sides of the pan with lady finger halves. Alternately add two layers each of the pudding and the lady fingers. Chill the pan in the refrigerator for 2 or 3 hours until the cake is set. Remove the cake from the pan. Garnish the cake with the remaining whipped cream and a few toasted almonds or walnuts, if desired. Serves 6 to 8.

Pound Cakes
Chapter 9

DE LUXE POUND CAKE

2 cups (1 lb.) country or
           dairy butter
2 cups (1 lb.) granulated
           sugar
9 eggs
1 tsp. vanilla

½ tsp. mace
4 cups (1 lb.) all-purpose
           flour, sifted
½ tsp. salt
½ tsp. cream of tartar

Cream the butter and sugar together well. Beat in the eggs, one at a time; beat after each addition. Add in the vanilla and the mace.

Sift the flour before measuring it, then resift it with the salt and cream of tartar. Mix the flour into the creamed mixture until it is thoroughly blended.

Pour the batter into a greased and floured 10 × 4-inch tube pan lined with heavy wax paper that should also be lightly greased. Bake in a slow oven at 325° for about 1 hour.

(Pound cakes need no icing and can be stored for a long time if they are thoroughly sealed in aluminum foil and placed in the refrigerator).

HOLIDAY POUND CAKE

1 lb. country or dairy butter
2½ cups granulated sugar
1 Tbsp. vanilla
1 tsp. grated lemon rind
9 large eggs
1 cup chopped, candied red
cherries

1 cup chopped, candied green
cherries
1 cup chopped pecans
4½ cups all-purpose flour,
sifted
1½ tsp. salt

Butter and flour the bottom of a 10 × 4-inch tube pan, and line it with lightly greased wax paper. Set it aside.

Cream the butter until it is fluffy and soft. Add the sugar gradually, beating thoroughly. Blend in the vanilla and the lemon rind. Add the eggs, one at a time, beating well after each.

Toss the cherries and nuts with 1 cup of the flour. Sift the remaining flour with the salt and fold it into the batter, ½ cup at a time, mixing until smooth. Lastly fold in the cherries and the nuts.

Bake for 1 hour and 45 minutes in a 325° oven. Cool the pan on a wire rack for at least 10 minutes before turning the cake out onto a platter.

This cake will keep several weeks if stored in a tightly covered container.

THRIFTY POUND CAKE

3 cups all-purpose flour, sifted
½ tsp. baking soda
½ tsp. baking powder
¾ tsp. salt
1 cup shortening

2 cups granulated sugar
4 eggs, unbeaten
1 tsp. lemon extract
1 tsp. vanilla
1 cup milk

Sift the flour, the soda, the baking power, and the salt together.

In another bowl cream the shortening with the sugar. Add in the unbeaten eggs, one at a time, then the extracts; now beat thoroughly. Then add in the flour mixture alternately with the milk.

Pour the batter into a greased and floured 9 × 5 × 3-inch loaf pan, lined with lightly greased wax paper, and bake in a 350° oven for about 1 hour and 10 minutes. Turn the cake out of the pan and remove the paper. Cool it on a rack.

MARBLE CAKE

1 stick butter	¼ tsp. salt
1½ cups granulated sugar	⅔ cup condensed milk
2 eggs	1½ tsp. vanilla
3 cups all-purpose flour, sifted	½ cup cocoa
3½ tsp. baking powder	2 Tbsp. condensed milk

Cream together the butter and sugar until they are light and fluffy. Beat in the 2 eggs vigorously. Mix the flour with the baking powder and the salt and add it alternately to the butter with the milk and the vanilla.

Put ⅓ of the batter into a second bowl. Add to this the cocoa and the 2 Tbsp. milk. Mix thoroughly.

Put the light and dark batters alternately by spoonsful into a greased and floured 9-inch tube pan. Bake in a 350° oven for about 1 hour, or until the cake shrinks from the sides of the pan. Invert the cake onto a cake rack and let it remain there in the pan until it is thoroughly cool. When the cake is cool, ice it with Fudge Frosting, (See p. 163).

HILDA BRACEY'S POUND CAKE

1 lb. granulated sugar (2 cups)	1 lb. eggs (8 medium eggs)
1 lb. country or dairy butter (room temperature)	1 lb. all-purpose flour, sifted (4 cups)

Cream together the sugar and butter.

Preheat the oven to 325°.

Add in the eggs and flour alternately, a small amount at a time, beating only enough to combine the ingredients completely.

Pour the batter into a greased and floured 11 × 7-inch loaf pan. Bake the cake for 1 hour.

Cool the cake in the pan for 10 minutes before turning it out onto a wire rack to finish cooling.

ICED SOUR CREAM POUND CAKE

2 sticks butter, softened	1 cup light sour cream
2½ cups granulated sugar	1 tsp. flavoring (vanilla, lemon or orange, or all three blended
6 eggs	
3 cups cake flour, sifted	
½ tsp. baking soda	Candied red cherries (for decorating)

Cream the butter with the sugar until they are light. Add the eggs, one at a time, beating thoroughly after each.

Sift the flour and soda 3 times and add them alternately with the sour cream into the first mixture, beating until the batter is quite smooth. Add the flavoring. Mix well.

Pour the batter into a 9-inch greased and floured tube pan, lined with lightly greased wax paper. Bake in a moderate oven at 350° for 1 hour and 20 minutes, or until a toothpick proves the cake is done.

Let the cake stand in the pan on a rack for about 5 minutes. Then turn it out and peel off the paper. Let the cake cool and then top it with a favorite icing, letting the icing run down the sides of the cake. Decorate with whole red cherries. Store the cake in an airtight box.

BASIC POUND CAKE

2 sticks country or dairy butter	2 cups cake flour, sifted
	½ tsp. salt
2 cups granulated sugar	2 tsp. vanilla
6 eggs	

Cream the butter and sugar together well.

Add the eggs, one at a time, alternately with tablespoons of flour. Combine well. Add in the salt and the vanilla.

Bake for about 50 minutes in a 9 × 5-inch greased and floured loaf pan in a preheated oven at 350°.

ENGLISH LEMON POUND CAKE

1 cup shortening	¼ tsp. yellow coloring
2 cups granulated sugar	½ tsp. salt
4 eggs	3 cups cake flour, sifted
1 Tbsp. lemon flavoring	¾ cup buttermilk
½ tsp. vanilla	1 tsp. baking soda
1 tsp. butter flavoring	1 Tbsp. vinegar

Cream the shortening with the sugar and add in the eggs one at a time. Mix well. Then add in the flavorings, the coloring, and the salt.

Sift the flour and add it in alternately with the buttermilk to the creamed mixture. Mix the soda and the vinegar in a small bowl and add them into the mixture. Blend well.

Bake in a 10 × 5-inch loaf pan that has been greased and lightly dusted with flour, in a slow oven at 325° for about 1 hour and 15 minutes, or until the toothpick test proves it done. Do not overbake.

CHOCOLATE LOAF CAKE

2 sticks margarine
2 cups granulated sugar
2½ cups cake flour, sifted
1 tsp. salt
1 tsp. baking soda
1 tsp. vanilla
4 eggs
1 cup buttermilk
3 (1 oz.) envelopes un-
   sweetened chocolate product
1 cup nuts, chopped

Cream together the margarine and the sugar. Sift the flour with the salt and soda and add it to the creamed mixture. Stir in the vanilla. Add one egg at a time, beating well after each addition. Add in the milk and mix thoroughly. Now add the chocolate product and blend; then stir in the nuts.

Bake in a lightly greased and floured 9 × 5-inch loaf pan lined with lightly greased wax paper at 350° for about 55 minutes.

Serve the cake plain or frosted with Butter Frosting, (See p. 160).

RAISIN WALNUT POUND CAKE

2¼ cups all-purpose flour,
                    sifted
1 cup chopped raisins
1½ tsp. cinnamon
¾ tsp. ground cloves
½ tsp. baking powder
¼ tsp. baking soda
¼ tsp. salt
1¼ sticks butter or margarine
1½ cups granulated sugar
3 eggs
¾ cup buttermilk
¾ cup chopped walnuts
2 Tbsp. grated orange peel

Preheat the oven to 350°. Lightly grease and flour a 9 × 5 × 3-inch loaf pan. Line the bottom of the pan with lightly greased wax paper.

Remove 2 Tbsp. of the flour and toss it with the raisins to coat them well. Sift the rest of the flour with the spices, the baking powder, salt, and the soda. Set this aside.

In a large bowl cream the sugar and butter together until they are light. Add in the eggs; beat again. Now beat the flour mixture into the creamed butter-egg mixture alternately with the buttermilk. Stir in the raisins, the walnuts and the orange peel.

Turn the batter into the prepared pan. Bake for 1 hour and 15 minutes, or until the cake tests done with a toothpick. Cool the cake in the pan on a wire rack for 10 minutes. Then turn it out, right side up, on the rack and let it cool completely. Sprinkle powdered sugar on top of the cake if desired.

SOUR CREAM CHOCOLATE CAKE

1 Tbsp. shortening	**1 tsp. salt**
1½ cups granulated sugar	**2 squares unsweetened**
1 cup light sour cream	**chocolate**
2 eggs	**¾ cup boiling water, scant**
2 cups cake flour, sifted	**1 tsp. vanilla**
1 tsp. baking soda	

Cream the shortening. Add a portion of the sugar, then add the cream and the rest of the sugar, mixing thoroughly. Beat the eggs and add them in.

Sift the flour; measure it. Add in the soda and the salt, and sift it again. Melt the chocolate and dilute it with the boiling water. Put the flour and the chocolate mix alternately into the batter. Mix thoroughly. Stir in the vanilla.

Pour the batter into a greased and floured 9 × 5-inch loaf pan. Bake in a 350° oven for about 35 to 40 minutes.

HALF-A-POUND CAKE

½ lb. cake flour	**½ lb. butter, softened**
(2¼ cups, sifted)	**(2 sticks)**
1 tsp. baking powder	**½ lb. eggs (4 eggs)**
¼ tsp. salt	**2 tsp. rose water**
¼ tsp. nutmeg	**½ lb. granulated sugar**
	(1 cup)

Sift the flour; resift it three times with the baking powder, the salt, and the nutmeg.

Cream the butter thoroughly; add in the flour mixture in three portions, mixing smooth after each addition.

Beat the eggs until they are thick and lemon colored. Add the flavorings and the sugar all at once and beat until the mixture is very light.

Combine the flour mixture and egg mixture, beating thoroughly.

Line a 9 × 5 × 3-inch pan with 4 thicknesses of smooth brown wrapping paper, the first (inmost) to be buttered. Pour in the batter, pushing it well into the corners of the pan. Then lay another piece of buttered brown paper across the top of the pan.

Bake in a 350° oven for ½ hour, then remove the paper from the top and bake one hour longer.

Cool the cake in the pan for 10 minutes before turning it out onto a wire cake rack to finish cooling.

(from Meta Given's MODERN FAMILY COOK BOOK)

SPICED LEMON POUND CAKE

4 cups all-purpose flour, sifted	2 cups granulated sugar
4 tsp. baking powder	6 eggs
1 tsp. ground mace	1 tsp. grated lemon rind
1 tsp. salt	1 cup milk
2 sticks butter or margarine	

Sift the flour, the baking powder, the mace and the salt together.

Cream the butter and gradually add in the sugar. Beat until the mixture is light and fluffy. Add in the eggs, one at a time, beating after each addition. Put in the grated lemon rind.

Now add in the flour mixture alternately with the milk. Beat the batter smooth. Pour the batter into a greased and floured 10 × 4-inch tube pan. Bake in a preheated oven at 325° for 1 hour and 15 minutes, or until the cake tests done with the toothpick test.

❧ Cupcakes
Chapter 10

QUICKLY MIXED CUPCAKES

2 cups cake flour, sifted
1⅓ cups ganulated sugar
¾ tsp. salt
½ cup shortening

1 cup milk
1 tsp. baking powder
2 eggs, beaten
1 tsp. vanilla

Combine the flour, sugar, salt, shortening, and ⅔ cup of milk. Beat two minutes by hand or in a mixer. Add the baking powder, the final ⅓ cup of milk, the eggs and the vanilla. Beat for two more minutes.

Fill greased and floured muffin tins one-half full. Bake in a hot oven at 400° for 20 minutes.

When the cupcakes are cool, cover them with your favorite icing. This recipe makes 16 cakes.

APPLESAUCE CUPCAKES

1 stick butter
1 cup granulated sugar
1 tsp. baking soda
1 cup applesauce
2 cups all-purpose flour, sifted
1 tsp. ground cloves

1 tsp. nutmeg
2 tsp. cinnamon
¼ cup buttermilk
½ cup chopped nutmeats
½ cup seeded raisins
2 Tbsp. brown sugar

Cream the butter and the white sugar together. Dissolve the soda in the applesauce and add them to the creamed mixture; blend well together.

Sift the flour with the cloves, the nutmeg and 1 tsp. of cinnamon and add to the batter along with the buttermilk. Beat all together smoothly. Add in the nutmeats and the raisins.

Grease and lightly flour muffin tins and fill them half full. Mix the brown sugar with the remaining tsp. of cinnamon and sprinkle on top. Bake in a 425° oven for about 20 minutes.

Makes about 20 cupcakes.

OATMEAL DATE CUPCAKES

1 cup all-purpose flour, sifted	½ cup chopped dates
¼ cup granulated sugar	3 Tbsp. cooking oil
3 tsp. baking powder	1 egg, beaten
½ tsp. salt	¾ cup milk
1 cup rolled oats, uncooked (quick or oldfashioned)	6 pitted dates, sliced in half lengthwise

Sift together the flour, sugar, baking powder and the salt. Stir in the oats and the chopped dates. Add the oil, the egg and the milk. Stir only until the dry ingredients are moistened.

Fill greased and floured muffin cups ⅔ full. Place ½ date on the batter in each muffin cup. Bake in a preheated hot oven, 425°, for about 15 minutes.

Frost the cakes with one-half the recipe for Orange Cream Frosting, (See p. 165). Makes 12 medium-sized cupcakes.

LOW CALORIE CUPCAKES

1 cup all-purpose flour, sifted	3 Tbsp. cooking oil
1 tsp. baking soda	2 eggs
½ tsp. salt	¾ cup buttermilk
½ tsp. nutmeg	1 cup rolled oats, uncooked (quick or oldfashioned)
1 tsp. cinnamon	¼ cup raisins
⅓ cup brown sugar	

Sift together the flour, soda, salt, and the spices into a bowl. Add the sugar, cooking oil, eggs, and about half the buttermilk. Beat until the mixture is smooth. Fold in the remaining buttermilk, the oats, and the raisins. Mix gently.

Fill small paper baking cups or small greased and floured muffin cups one-half full. Bake in a 375° oven for 12 to 15 minutes. This recipe makes 20 small cakes.

Unfrosted these cupcakes equal 82 calories each.

SPICY CUPCAKES

1 stick butter	1 tsp. cinnamon
1 cup brown sugar	1 tsp. nutmeg
1 egg	1 tsp. ground cloves
1 cup sour milk	1 cup raisins
2 cups all-purpose flour, sifted	½ cup chopped nut meats
1 tsp. soda	

Blend the butter with the sugar. Add the egg and stir it in. Add in the sour milk.

Sift the flour, soda and spices together and add them to the creamed mixture. Finally, add the raisins and the nuts. Mix well.

Bake in greased and floured muffin tins for 15 minutes in a 350° oven. Place about 3 Tbsp. of batter in each muffin cup. When done, top cakes with Uncooked Icing, (See p. 175).

Yield, about 16 cupcakes.

VANILLA CUPCAKES

1 stick butter	½ tsp. salt
1 cup granulated sugar	1 tsp. baking powder
2 eggs	1 cup milk
2 cups all-purpose flour, sifted	1 tsp. vanilla

Cream together the sugar and the butter. Beat the eggs until they foam and add them to the first mixture.

Sift the flour, the salt and baking powder together and add it into the creamed mixture alternately with the milk. Stir thoroughly. Put in the vanilla and beat again.

Bake in greased and floured muffin tins for 15 to 20 minutes at 425°.

Makes about 20 medium-sized cakes. Top with a favorite icing if desired.

BUTTERMILK CUPCAKES

⅛ stick butter	1½ cups cake flour, sifted
1 cup granulated sugar	½ tsp. baking soda
1 egg, beaten	1 cup buttermilk
½ tsp. lemon extract	14 pecan halves

Cream the butter and the sugar together. Add in the beaten egg and the extract. Blend thoroughly. Sift into the batter the flour and the soda, adding in the milk alternately as you sift.

Pour the batter into greased and floured cupcake pans and bake in a 375° oven for 25 minutes. If the pans are filled about half full this batter will make 14 cupcakes.

Frost with Brown Sugar Icing, No. 2 (See p. 170) and place a pecan half on top of each cake.

PINK CUPCAKES

½ cup shortening	1 tsp. vanilla
1 cup granulated sugar	½ cup milk
2 cups cake flour, sifted	3 egg whites
½ tsp. salt	Red cake coloring
2 tsp. baking powder	

Cream the shortening thoroughly, then add in the sugar gradually; cream the mixture until it is light and fluffy.

Sift the flour, the salt, and the baking powder together. Mix the vanilla into the milk and add it alternately with the combined dry ingredients into the sugar mixture. Beat with a spoon after each addition until the mixture is smooth.

Beat the egg whites stiff but not dry and fold them carefully into the batter. Put enough red cake coloring into the batter to make the cake a delicate pink. Then divide the batter into 24 greased and lightly floured cupcake pans. (You can use small paper cups placed inside of muffin tins.) Bake for 20 to 30 minutes in a 375° oven.

When the cakes are cool, frost them with your favorite white icing.

SUNSHINE CUPCAKES

For these cakes use the same ingredients called for in the Pink Cup Cakes (See P. 109), except that, only ¼ cup of milk should be used. And instead of the egg whites, use 3 egg yolks beaten until thick and lemon-colored.

Frost with your favorite icing and color bright-red if desired.

℞ Cakes for Party Giving and Party Going—At Home, Church and Club
Chapter 11

ST. NICK'S CAKE

½ cup shortening
1½ cups granulated sugar
2 eggs
2 Tbsp. cocoa
2-oz. red food coloring
1 tsp. vanilla
1 cup buttermilk

1 tsp. salt
2½ cups cake flour, sifted
1 tsp. baking soda
1 tsp. vinegar
1 Tbsp. green food coloring
10 maraschino cherries, quartered

Cream the shortening and the sugar together smoothly. Add in the eggs. Make a paste of the cocoa and the red food coloring and beat it into the first mixture. Stir the vanilla into the buttermilk; mix the salt into the flour; add these alternately into the shortening mixture. Dissolve the soda in the vinegar and stir this gently into the batter.

Bake in two greased and floured 9-inch layer cake pans in a 350° oven for 30 minutes. Cool on a wire rack.

Frost with Uncooked Icing (See p. 175), tinted green with the green coloring. Decorate with the cherries.

CHILD'S RAINBOW BIRTHDAY CAKE

1⅜ sticks butter

1½ cups granulated sugar

1 cup milk or water

¼ tsp. salt

3 cups cake flour, sifted

4 tsp. baking powder

3 egg whites, beaten stiffly

1 tsp. vanilla

Green coloring

Pink coloring

1 egg yolk

Cream the butter, add in the sugar gradually, and cream again. Add in the milk or water.

Sift the salt into 2½ cups of flour and fold it into the creamed mix. Beat thoroughly. Sift the baking powder into the remaining ½ cup of flour; fold this in now. Finally, cut and fold in the egg whites and the vanilla.

Divide the batter into three portions. To one portion add the green coloring. To another portion add the pink coloring. To the third portion add the egg yolk.

Bake in three greased and floured 8-inch layer cake pans in a moderately hot oven at 375° for 25 to 30 minutes. When the layers are cool, put them together with a white icing and decorate with colored jelly beans.

ST. PATRICK'S DAY CAKE

1½ cups granulated sugar

¾ cup shortening

3 cups cake flour, sifted

½ tsp. salt

2½ tsp. baking powder

6 egg whites

1 cup milk

1 tsp. vanilla

¼ tsp. almond extract

Cream together the sugar and the shortening. Sift the flour once, then sift it again with the salt and the baking powder. Place the sugar and the shortening in a bowl and add the unbeaten egg whites and 4 Tbsp. of the milk. Beat together thoroughly. Add the extracts, then the flour, alternately with the remaining milk. Beat vigorously.

Bake in a 9-inch greased and floured tube pan for 45 to 50 minutes, in a 350° oven.

Frost with Basic Boiled Icing, (See p. 169), then cover with Green Tinted Coconut, (See p. 177).

CRYSTAL CAKE

2¼ cups cake flour, sifted	1 tsp. vanilla
1½ cups granulated sugar	1 cup milk
4 tsp. baking powder	1 tsp. orange extract
1 tsp. salt	4 egg whites, unbeaten
½ cup shortening	

Sift together the flour, sugar, baking powder and salt; add the shortening, the vanilla, ¾ cup of milk, and the orange extract. Beat well. Add in the egg whites, then ¼ cup of milk, and beat again.

Pour the batter into 2 greased and floured 8-inch layer cake pans. Bake in a moderate 350° oven until the cake tests done (about 30 to 35 minutes). Cool the cake, then remove it from the pans.

Spread between the layers and on top of the cake with Hula Frosting, (See p. 163).

JOANNE SNIDER'S BIRTHDAY CAKE

2 cups all-purpose flour, sifted	Grated rind of 1 orange
1 tsp. baking soda	2 eggs, separated
⅛ tsp. salt	1 tsp. vanilla
1 stick butter	⅔ cup buttermilk (or
1 cup granulated sugar	sour milk)

Sift, then measure the flour. Sift it three times with the soda and the salt.

Cream the butter until it is lemon colored; gradually add in the sugar, beating after each addition. Add the grated rind. Beat the egg yolks and add them in. Then add in the vanilla. Blend well. Next, add in the sifted dry ingredients alternately with the milk.

Beat the egg whites and fold them gently into the batter.

Turn the batter into a greased and floured 9-inch square pan lined with lightly greased wax paper. Bake at 350° for about 45 minutes.

When the cake is cool, frost it with Orange Coconut Frosting, (See p. 165).

BANANA NUT CAKE

3 cups cake flour, sifted	**1 cup milk**
¾ tsp. salt	**1 tsp. vanilla**
4 tsp. baking powder	**3 bananas (more or less,**
1½ sticks butter	**according to size)**
1½ cups granulated sugar	**½ cup chopped nuts**
3 eggs, separated	

Mix and sift the flour, salt, and the baking powder together three times. Cream the butter and add the sugar gradually; cream thoroughly. Then beat the egg yolks and add them to the creamed mixture. Beat this mixture until it is fluffy. Next add in the milk gradually, and the vanilla.

Beat the egg whites stiffly and fold them into the batter.

Bake in two greased and floured 9-inch or three 7-inch layer cake pans in a 375° oven for about 30 minutes. While the cake is baking, make Brown Sugar Icing No. 1, (See p. 169).

When the cake is cool, put slices of banana over the first layer, spread on icing, put on the next layer and cover with bananas and icing as before. Cover the top layer with bananas and the chopped nuts. Put the remainder of the icing on the sides of the cake.

POPPY SEED CAKE

½ cup shortening	**¼ tsp. salt**
1½ cups granulated sugar	**1¼ cups milk**
⅔ cup poppy seeds	**1 tsp. almond extract**
2 cups all-purpose flour, sifted	**3 egg whites**
3½ tsp. baking powder	

Cream the shortening with the sugar well; add in the poppy seeds. Stir well.

Sift the flour with the baking powder and the salt and add it to the creamed mixture alternately with the milk. Then add in the extract.

Beat the egg whites lightly and fold them into the batter.

Bake in two greased and floured 9-inch layer cake pans at 360° for 25 to 30 minutes.

When the cake has cooled, ice it with Vanilla Marshmallow Frosting, (See p. 168).

STRAWBERRY MERINGUE CAKE

2 cups cake flour, sifted	4 egg yolks, beaten
4 tsp. baking powder	¾ cup milk
¾ tsp. salt	1 tsp. vanilla
1 stick butter	4 egg whites, stiffly beaten
2 cups granulated sugar	1 qt. fresh strawberries

Sift the flour once and measure it; add the baking powder and salt and sift all together 3 times.

Cream the butter; add 1 cup of sugar gradually and cream together until the mix is light and fluffy. Add the egg yolks, then the sifted flour alternately with the milk, a small quantity at a time. Beat after each addition. Add the vanilla.

Bake in two 9-inch greased and floured layer cake pans in a 375° oven for 25 minutes. Allow the cake to cool.

Fold ½ cup of sugar slowly into the beaten egg whites. Place the two cake layers on a baking sheet, pile the egg white meringue on them and place them in a moderate oven to brown the meringue.

Prepare the berries (reserving a few as a garnish) by crushing them with ½ cup of sugar. Spread the berry mix gently on top of the meringue and put the layers together. Garnish the top of the cake with the whole berries. Serve at once.

MARASCHINO CHERRY CAKE

2¾ cups cake flour, sifted	⅔ cup milk
1¾ cups granulated sugar	16 maraschino cherries
1 tsp. salt	⅔ cup unbeaten egg whites
4 tsp. baking powder	(about five)
1¼ sticks butter	½ cup chopped nuts
⅓ cup juice (from cherries)	

Sift together the flour, sugar, salt, and baking powder into a bowl. Add the butter, the cherry juice, the milk and the cherries, cut into eighths. Beat vigorously for 2 minutes. Add the unbeaten egg whites and continue beating for about 3 minutes longer. Fold in the chopped nuts.

Pour the batter into two greased and floured 9-inch layer cake pans, and bake for 30 to 35 minutes at 350°.

When cake is cool frost with Snow White Frosting, (See p. 167) using cherry juice instead of water. Decorate with bright red cherries.

APPLE PRESERVE CAKE

¾ cup shortening	1 tsp. baking powder
1 cup granulated sugar	½ tsp. allspice
¼ cup light sour cream	1 tsp. cinnamon
½ cup apple preserves	½ tsp. nutmeg
3 eggs	½ cup chopped walnut meats
2 cups cake flour, sifted	½ cup seedless raisins
1 tsp. baking soda	

Cream the shortening and the sugar together until they are fluffy. Add the cream and apple preserves, mixing well. Add the eggs, 1 at a time.

Sift the flour, soda, baking powder and spices together three times; add them gradually into the liquid mixture. Roll the nuts and raisins in a little flour and fold them in.

Pour the batter into a greased and floured 8 × 4-inch loaf pan and bake at 350° for 50 minutes. Or bake in two 9-inch layer pans for 25 to 30 minutes.

Ice with Lemon Cream Butter Icing, (See p. 173).

CHOCOLATE BUTTER CAKE

3 squares unsweetened choco- late	1 stick butter
2¼ cups cake flour, sifted	1¼ cups granulated sugar
½ tsp. salt	3 eggs
3 tsp. baking powder	1 tsp. vanilla
	1¼ cups milk

Melt the chocolate and set it aside to cool. Sift the flour, salt and baking powder together. Cream the butter and sugar together and to them add one egg at a time, beating well after each addition. Stir in the vanilla. Now add the sifted dry ingredients alternately with the milk and the chocolate.

Pour the batter into two greased and floured 9-inch layer cake pans. Bake in a 350° oven for 30 to 35 minutes.

Cool the cake on cake rack and frost with Butter Frosting, (See p. 160), substituting 1 drop of peppermint flavoring for the vanilla called for in that recipe. If desired, tint the icing a pale pink with two drops of red cake coloring. Garnish with crushed peppermint stick candy.

SILVERY MOON CAKE

1¼ sticks butter	¾ tsp. salt
2 cups granulated sugar	1 cup milk
3 tsp. baking powder	5 egg whites
3 cups cake flour, sifted	

Cream the butter with the sugar.

Sift the baking powder with the flour and the salt and add it to the butter blend alternately with the milk.

Beat the egg whites, not too stiffly, then fold them into the batter.

Bake in two 9-inch greased and floured layer cake pans in a 375° oven for 20 to 35 minutes. Fill with Lemon Custard Filling, (See p. 159).

SPANISH LAYER CAKE

⅓ cup shortening	¼ tsp. ground cloves
1 cup granulated sugar	¼ tsp. salt
1⅞ cups cake flour, sifted	½ cup milk
3 tsp. baking powder	2 eggs, separated
1 tsp. cinnamon	½ cup raspberry jam

Cream together the shortening and the sugar. Mix and sift the flour, baking powder, spices and salt together; add these to the first mixture alternately with the milk.

Beat the egg whites stiffly and cut and fold them in. Blend in the egg yolks.

Bake in two well-greased and lightly floured 8-inch layer cake pans at 350° for 45 minutes.

When the cake has cooled, spread the raspberry jam between the layers and cover the top with a white frosting of your choice.

RUDDY DEVIL'S FOOD CAKE

2 cups cake flour, sifted	2 eggs, unbeaten
½ tsp. salt	1 tsp. vanilla
⅓ cup cocoa	1½ tsp. red food coloring
1 Tbsp. instant coffee	½ cup buttermilk
1½ cups granulated sugar	1½ tsp. baking soda
½ cup shortening	¾ cup boiling water

Sift together the flour, salt, cocoa and instant coffee and set aside. Gradually add the sugar to the shortening, creaming well. Beat in the eggs, one at a time. Add the vanilla and the food coloring. Add alternately and gradually the sifted dry ingredients and the buttermilk, beating smooth after each addition. Mix the soda into the boiling water and add them to the batter. Blend in.

Pour the thin batter into a greased and floured 9 × 5-inch pan lined with lightly greased wax paper and bake at 350° for 30 to 35 minutes, or until tested done with a toothpick.

Turn the cake out on a wire rack and peel off the wax paper. Frost when it is cool with Snow White Frosting, (See p. 167) or Chocolate Butter Icing, (See p. 171).

APPLE SURPRISE CAKE

2 cups chopped tart apples	½ cup cooking oil
1 cup granulated sugar	1 egg, beaten
1½ cups all-purpose flour, sifted	1 tsp. lemon extract
½ tsp. salt	½ cup chopped nuts
1 tsp. baking powder	1 cup flaked coconut

Chop the apples and pour the sugar over them. Let them stand until juice forms.

Sift the flour, salt and baking powder together and add them to the apple mixture. Add in the remaining ingredients.

Bake in a greased and floured 9-inch tube pan, at 350° for 30 minutes. This cake needs no icing but use one if you wish.

PRUNE CAKE

1½ cups all-purpose flour, sifted
½ tsp. ground cloves
½ tsp. cinnamon
1 cup granulated sugar
½ cup shortening

2 eggs
1 tsp. baking soda
4 Tbsp. sour milk
1 cup cooked prunes, chopped

Sift together the flour and the spices.
Cream the sugar with the shortening. Add in the eggs.
Dissolve the soda in the sour milk.
Add in the dry ingredients alternately with the sour milk mix into the sugar mixture. Lastly, add in the prunes.
Bake in two greased and floured 8-inch layer cake pans at 375° for 30 minutes. Fill the layers with Prune Nut Filling, (See p. 160).

COLONIAL FRUIT CAKE

3 cups cake flour, sifted
1½ tsp. baking powder
½ tsp. salt
1½ sticks butter
2 cups granulated sugar
4 eggs, separated
1 cup milk

½ tsp. vanilla
2 tsp. cinnamon
½ cup currants
½ cup chopped, moist citron
½ tsp. ground cloves
½ tsp. nutmeg

Measure the flour; sift it three times with the baking powder and salt. Cream the butter with the sugar well. Beat the egg yolks lightly and add them to the creamed mixture. Then add the sifted flour mixture alternately with the milk. Beat the egg whites stiffly and fold them in.

Divide the batter in half. Add the vanilla to one half; to the second half, add the fruit and the spices. Stir each gently. Bake each half in an 8-inch greased and floured square pan lined with lightly greased wax paper in a 350° oven, the white layer about 30 minutes, the dark layer 35 minutes. Cool the cake.

Put the spice layer on the bottom and spread with Snow White Frosting, (See p. 167). Add the white layer on top and cover the whole cake with the rest of the frosting.

RICH SOFT HONEY CAKE

½ stick butter or margarine
¼ cup shortening
1 cup strained honey
1 egg, well beaten
½ cup buttermilk

4 cups cake flour, sifted
1 tsp. baking soda
½ tsp. salt
½ tsp. cinnamon

Cream together thoroughly the butter, shortening, honey, and the egg. Pour in the buttermilk; blend well. Sift the flour with the soda, salt and cinnamon and fold into the first mixture. Mix well and bake in a greased and floured pan, 13 × 9 × 2-inches, in a 350° oven for 50 minutes.

When cool the cake may be cut and served in square brownie-like pieces, or sliced in half to form a 2-layer cake and frosted with icing.

HOLIDAY CAKE

½ yeast cake
½ cup lukewarm water
2½ cups all-purpose flour,
                    sifted
½ tsp. granulated sugar
1 stick butter
1 cup brown sugar
1 egg, beaten

½ cup milk
1 tsp. cinnamon
¼ tsp. ground cloves
¼ tsp. nutmeg
1 tsp. salt
1 cup chopped raisins
½ cup chopped figs or dates

Soften the yeast in the lukewarm water; add ½ cup of flour and the white sugar and beat well. Put this aside in a warm place to rise for about an hour.

Meantime, cream the butter and brown sugar, add the beaten egg and the milk. Sift together the flour, the spices and the salt. Then combine all the ingredients, including the yeast mixture, and mix well.

Pour the batter into a well-greased and lightly floured 9 or 10-inch tube pan. Cover it with a cloth and place it in a warm place to rise for 3 or 4 hours.

Bake for 1 hour in a moderate oven at 350°.

MIDNIGHT MALLOW CAKE

¼ lb. marshmallows (16)
3 squares unsweetened choco-
                        late
¾ cup boiling water
2¼ cups cake flour, sifted
1½ tsp. baking soda

¼ tsp. salt
3 eggs, well beaten
1¼ cups light sour cream
1¼ cups granulated sugar
1 cup chopped nuts

Melt the marshmallows and the chocolate in a double boiler over hot water. Add the ¾ cup of boiling water; beat until smooth. Let this mixture cool.

Sift the flour, soda and salt together. Add in the marshmallow-chocolate mixture. Then put in the eggs, the cream and the sugar. Add the nuts last. Mix thoroughly.

Pour the batter into two greased and floured 9-inch layer cake pans. Bake in a 375° oven for 25 to 30 minutes. Cool the cake and frost it with Vanilla Marshmallow Frosting, (See p. 168).

CHEESY DUTCH APPLE CAKE

2 cups all-purpose flour, sifted
½ cup granulated sugar
1½ tsp. baking powder
1 tsp. salt
½ stick butter

1½ cups shredded cheddar
                        cheese
1 egg, beaten
¾ cup milk
2 medium-sized tart apples

Sift together the flour, sugar, baking powder and salt. Cut in the butter until the mixture resembles coarse meal. Add the cheese and toss lightly to blend with the dry ingredients. Combine the egg and the milk; add to the dry ingredients and stir until blended. Spread the batter evenly in a buttered and floured 9-inch square pan.

Pare, quarter and core the apples and cut them into ¼-inch slices. Press the apple slices diagonally into the dough, with rounded edges up, about ½ inch apart. Bake for 35 minutes at 375°. Meanwhile prepare the glaze.

Glaze

¾ **cup granulated sugar**	½ **stick butter**
½ **tsp. cinnamon**	**1 Tbsp. lemon juice**
⅓ **cup water**	

In a saucepan blend the sugar and the cinnamon. Add the water, butter, and lemon juice, and bring to a boil. Remove the pan from the heat and allow contents to cool slightly. Remove the cake from the oven. Pour the glaze over the cake, loosening the edges to let the glaze run down between the cake and the sides of the pan. Return the pan to the oven and bake 15 minutes or until the cake is well browned and the apples are soft. Serve this cake while warm, topped with Lemon Raisin Sauce, (See p. 178). Makes 9 to 12 servings.

SWEET BUTTERMILK CAKE

3 cups cake flour, sifted	**1 tsp. vanilla**
¾ tsp. baking soda	**1 tsp. lemon extract**
2 tsp. baking powder	**1 tsp. orange extract**
1 stick butter	**1½ cups buttermilk**
1½ cups granulated sugar	**2 eggs**

Sift the flour, soda and baking powder together.

Cream the butter with the sugar. Add the vanilla, lemon and orange extracts. Add in the sifted dry ingredients alternately with the buttermilk. Beat in the eggs gently. Mix well.

Pour the batter into two 9-inch round layer cake pans (or a 13 × 9-inch loaf pan) which have been greased and floured.

Bake in a 350° oven for 25 to 30 minutes (40 minutes may be required for the loaf pan).

Remove the cake from the pans and cool it on a cake rack. When it is cool, frost with Butter Frosting (See p. 160), and decorate as desired.

DANISH WHITE CAKE

½ cup shortening, or 1 stick butter
1 tsp. vanilla
1⅓ cups granulated sugar
2½ cups cake flour, sifted
¼ tsp. salt

2½ tsp. baking powder
1 cup milk
3 egg whites
½ cup raspberry jam
¼ pint heavy cream

Cream the shortening with the vanilla. Add in the sugar gradually and continue creaming until it is well mixed.

Sift the flour before measuring; sift it again with the salt and the baking powder. Add the flour mix alternately with the milk into the creamed sugar mixture. Whip the egg whites well and fold them into the batter.

Bake in two greased and floured 8-inch layer cake pans lined with lightly greased wax paper, for 30 minutes, in a 350° oven.

Spread jam between the cake layers. Whip the cream and flavor it with ½ teaspoon of either vanilla or almond extract. Spread the cream all over the outer surface of the cake.

FUDGE NUT CAKE

1¾ cups cake flour, sifted
2 cups granulated sugar
2 tsp. baking powder
¼ tsp. baking soda
1 tsp. salt
¼ cup shortening, softened

1½ cups milk
1 tsp. vanilla
2 eggs
4 squares unsweetened chocolate, melted
1 cup nut meats, cut up fine

Heat the oven to 350°. Grease and flour two round 8 or 9-inch layer cake pans.

Sift the flour, sugar, baking powder, soda, and the salt into a bowl. Add in the shortening, the milk, and the vanilla. Beat for 2 minutes.

Put in the eggs and the melted chocolate. Beat for two more minutes. Dredge the nuts lightly with a little flour and add them in.

Bake for 35 to 40 minutes. Cool the cake and ice it with Honey Butter Icing, (See p. 173).

HONEY NUT CAKE

2 cups cake flour, sifted	½ cup honey
2 tsp. baking powder	3 eggs
½ tsp. salt	1 cup finely cut nut meats
1⅜ sticks butter	¼ cup milk
½ cup granulated sugar	1 tsp. vanilla

Sift the flour once, then measure it; add in the baking powder and salt and sift together three times.

Cream the butter; add the sugar gradually to it and cream thoroughly. Add in the honey, one-half at a time, beating after each addition. Add in ½ cup of the flour mix and beat until the whole mixture is smooth and well blended.

Beat the eggs until they are thick enough to pile up in the bowl; add them to the cake mixture and beat well. Add the nuts. Now add in the remaining flour in thirds, alternately with the milk in halves, beating well after each addition. Finally, add the vanilla.

Bake in a greased and floured 9-inch tube pan in a slow oven, 325°, for 1 hour and 5 minutes.

Frost with Honey Frosting, (See p. 163), or serve plain.

AMBER CAKE

⅓ cup shortening	¼ tsp. salt
1½ cups granulated sugar	¾ cup water
2½ cups cake flour, sifted	½ tsp. almond extract
4 tsp. baking powder	4 egg yolks, beaten

Cream the shortening with the sugar. Mix and sift the flour, baking powder, and the salt; add these alternately to the first mixture with the water and the extract. Fold in the beaten egg yolks.

Bake in a greased and floured sheet (shallow pan about 13 × 9 inches) for 35 minutes in a 350° oven. When the cake is cool, cut it in half and put it together with Mocha Frosting, (See p. 164).

MAPLE SNOW CAKE

2¾ cups cake flour, sifted	2 eggs, separated
½ tsp. salt	1 cup hot water
½ cup shortening	4 tsp. baking powder
1½ cups granulated sugar	½ tsp. maple flavoring

Lightly grease and flour two 9-inch cake pans and line them with lightly greased wax paper.

Sift the flour and salt together. Cream the shortening with the sugar until they are light and fluffy. Beat the egg yolks and add them to the creamed mixture. Add in the sifted dry ingredients alternately with the water. Beat the egg whites well and add the baking powder to them. Fold into the mixture. Add the flavoring.

Pour the batter into the pans and bake in a moderate oven at 350° for 30 to 35 minutes. Cool the cake and frost it with Maple Icing, (See p. 173).

FROSTED MOCHA CAKE

½ cup shortening	1 tsp. baking powder
1½ cups granulated sugar	1 tsp. baking soda
2 eggs	½ tsp. salt
⅔ cup buttermilk	1 tsp. cinnamon
½ cup cold strong coffee	½ cup cocoa
1¾ cups cake flour, sifted	1 tsp. vanilla

Cream the shortening with the sugar; beat the eggs well and add them in. Blend well. Put in half the buttermilk and the coffee.

Sift together the flour, baking powder, the soda, salt, cinnamon and cocoa; add one-half of this mix to the creamed ingredients. Beat well. Then add the remaining buttermilk and flour, also the vanilla, and beat thoroughly.

Bake in two lightly greased and floured 9-inch layer cake pans at 350° for 30 to 35 minutes.

When the cake is cool spread on Mocha Frosting, (See p. 164).

CHOCOLATE NOUGAT CAKE

3 oz. unsweetened chocolate, cut very fine
½ cup boiling water
1¾ cups cake flour, sifted
1 cup granulated sugar
¾ tsp. salt
½ tsp. baking powder

¾ tsp. baking soda
½ cup shortening
½ cup dark corn syrup
⅓ cup sour milk
1 tsp. vanilla
2 eggs, unbeaten

Put the chocolate in a mixing bowl. Pour the boiling water slowly over it and stir until blended. Set aside to cool.

Sift the flour, sugar, salt, baking powder and soda into the chocolate mixture. Cream the shortening smoothly and add it in, then put in the corn syrup. Beat 200 strokes. Now add the milk, eggs and vanilla. Beat again thoroughly.

Bake in a 12 × 8 × 2-inch greased and floured pan in a 350° oven for 50 to 60 minutes.

Spread the top of the cake with Nougat Frosting, (See p. 164).

LARGE BIRTHDAY CAKE

3 cups all-purpose flour, sifted
3½ tsp. baking powder
¾ tsp. salt
1½ cups granulated sugar

½ cup shortening (softened)
5 egg yolks, unbeaten
1½ tsp. vanilla
1¼ cups milk

Sift together the flour, baking powder and salt. In another bowl, cream together the sugar and shortening with the unbeaten egg yolks and the vanilla. Beat for 2 minutes. Add the flour mixture to the sugar mixture alternately with the milk. Beat only enough to blend.

Pour the batter into two deep 9-inch greased and floured layer cake pans. Bake at 350° for about 35 minutes. Remove the cake from the pans. Let it cool.

Ice with a boiled icing. Sprinkle with coconut and chopped maraschino cherries, if desired.

SUE BREEDEN'S CHOCOLATE CAKE

1 (4-oz.) pkg. German's sweet chocolate
½ cup boiling water
2 cups granulated sugar
1 cup shortening
3 egg yolks, unbeaten
½ tsp. vanilla

1 Tbsp. lemon juice
2½ cups cake flour, sifted
1 tsp. baking soda
¼ tsp. salt
1⅛ cups milk
3 egg whites, stiffly beaten

Melt the chocolate in the boiling water. Allow it to cool. Cream the sugar with the shortening until they are light and fluffy. Add the egg yolks, one at a time, beating after each addition. Add the vanilla and the melted chocolate. Mix until blended. Blend in the lemon juice.

Sift together the flour, soda and the salt. Add these sifted dry ingredients to the chocolate mixture alternately with the milk. Beat after each addition until the batter is smooth. Then fold in the egg whites.

Pour the batter into three 9-inch greased and floured layer pans lined with lightly greased wax paper. Bake in a 350° oven for 35 to 40 minutes. Let the cake cool.

Frost the cake top and between the layers with Coconut Pecan Frosting, (See p. 162), or with whipped cream.

WEDDING CAKE

(Cakes for a large wedding should be made by a caterer or professional baker, but for a small, informal home wedding or a family wedding at the church, the mother of the bride or a close relative often wishes to bake the cake for sentimental reasons.)

1½ sticks butter
2 cups granulated sugar
1 cup sweet milk
3½ cups cake flour, sifted
⅛ tsp. salt

2 tsp. baking powder (heaped)
6 egg whites, well beaten
1 tsp. lemon extract

Cream the butter with the sugar; add in the milk. Sift the flour three times with the salt and the baking powder, and then add it into the milk mixture. Fold in the egg whites lightly and quickly, then the flavoring.

This cake can be baked in layers in graduated size greased and floured pans so as to make tiers. It should be baked until the toothpick test proves it done in a 350° oven, for about 30 to 35 minutes.

Put the layers together with a white icing, and decorate as desired. Serves 10 to 12.

If a larger cake is needed, the recipe should be repeated before baking (not doubled or tripled) for greater ease in handling, and for better results.

BRIDAL SHOWER CAKE

½ cup shortening	½ tsp. salt
2 cups granulated sugar	½ cup milk
2½ cups cake flour, sifted	1 tsp. orange extract
3 tsp. baking powder	Whites of 8 eggs

Cream the shortening; add the sugar gradually, beating constantly. Mix and sift the flour with the baking powder and the salt; add it alternately to the first mixture with the milk and continue beating. Add in the extract. Beat the egg whites stiff and dry and cut and fold them in.

Fill a 9-inch tube pan, well greased and lightly floured, with the batter and bake for 50 minutes in a 350° oven. When the cake is cool, spread on a white icing.

BLACKBERRY JAM CAKE

3 cups cake flour, sifted plus	2 sticks butter
1 Tbsp. cake flour	2 cups granulated sugar
½ tsp. salt	1 tsp. baking soda
1 tsp. cinnamon	1 cup buttermilk
¼ tsp. ground cloves	6 eggs
¼ tsp. allspice	2 cups seedless blackberry jam

Stir together the flour, the salt, and the spices.

Cream the butter and sugar together well, then add in the sifted flour mix. Blend well. Stir the soda into the buttermilk; add into the mixture. Stir again. Add in the eggs, one at a time, mixing well after each. Lastly, add the blackberry jam. Mix it in thoroughly.

Bake in three greased and floured 8-inch layer cake pans for 25 to 30 minutes at 350°. Frost with a lemon, white or caramel icing.

VANILLA MARSHMALLOW CAKE

2 cups all-purpose flour,
sifted
½ tsp. salt
2 tsp. baking powder
2 tsp. vanilla

1⅓ cups granulated sugar
⅔ cup shortening
3 large eggs
⅔ cup milk

Sift together the flour, salt, and the baking powder. Then blend the vanilla and the sugar into the shortening. Beat the eggs into the shortening mix, then stir in the flour mixture alternately with the milk. Beat the batter for ½ minute. Turn the batter into two well greased, lightly floured 9-inch layer cake pans.

Bake in a preheated moderate oven at 375° for 30 minutes, or until a toothpick inserted in the center comes out clean. Cool the cake on a wire rack. Spread the layers and the top of the cake with Vanilla Marshmallow Frosting, (See p. 168).

MARYLAND CAKE

2½ cups cake flour, sifted
1½ tsp. baking powder
½ tsp. salt
1 stick butter

1⅓ cups granulated sugar
1 tsp. vanilla
⅔ cup milk
4 egg whites

Measure the flour; sift it three times with the baking powder and the salt. Cream the butter with the sugar until they are smooth. Stir in the vanilla. Add the sifted dry ingredients alternately with the milk into the butter mix. Beat the egg whites stiffly and fold them in to the batter.

Bake in two greased and floured 8-inch layer cake pans lined with lightly greased wax paper at 375° for about 25 minutes. Let the cake cool.

Frost with Tutti Frutti Icing, (See p. 175).

BLACK WALNUT CAKE

½ cup shortening
1 cup granulated sugar
1¾ cups cake flour, sifted
2½ tsp. baking powder
¼ tsp. salt

½ cup coffee
½ cup milk
3 egg whites
¾ cup black walnut meats, chopped

Cream the shortening with the sugar. Sift the flour before measuring, then sift the flour, baking powder and salt together and add them alternately with the coffee and the milk into the creamed mixture. Beat the egg whites stiffly and fold them in. Add in the nuts.

Pour the batter into two greased and floured 7-inch layer pans (or a medium size loaf pan) lined with lightly greased wax paper. Bake at 350°, the layers for 30 minutes, as a loaf for 45 minutes.

Allow the cake to cool and frost it with a favorite icing.

VANILLA WAFER CAKE

1 stick margarine
1 cup granulated sugar
2 eggs
⅔ cup milk
½ tsp. salt
1 tsp. baking powder

1 tsp. vanilla
½ cup shredded coconut
2½ cups crumbled vanilla wafers
½ cup chopped nuts
Flour

Cream the margarine with the sugar. Mix together thoroughly the eggs and the milk. Sift in the salt and the baking powder. Blend all these ingredients in a mixing bowl. Stir into this mixture the vanilla, the coconut, and the vanilla wafers. Very lightly dust the nuts with flour and stir them in last.

Bake in a 350° oven in a 9 × 5-inch greased and floured loaf pan for 1 hour. Frost with Brown Sugar Icing No. 2, (See p. 170).

MAJESTIC CAKE

¾ cup shortening
1½ cups granulated sugar
4 eggs
3 cups all-purpose flour, sifted

3 tsp. baking powder
1½ tsp. salt
¾ cup milk
2 tsp. vanilla

For Filling

⅓ cups chopped candied cherries

½ cup chopped raisins
½ cup chopped nuts

Cream the shortening and the sugar together. Beat the eggs well and mix them well into the shortening mix. Mix and sift the flour, baking powder and the salt; add them alternately with the milk into the creamed mixture. Add in the vanilla, then beat thoroughly.

Bake in 3 greased and floured 9-inch layer cake pans in a 400° oven for 25 minutes. Mix the filling, and when the cake is cool, spread it between the layers of the cake. Then spread the sides and the top of the cake with Ornamental Frosting, (See p. 166).

CORAL SANFORD'S COMPANY CAKE

2½ cups unsweetened applesauce
3 tsp. baking soda
2 cups granulated sugar
2 sticks butter
4 cups all-purpose flour, sifted
½ tsp. nutmeg
½ tsp. cinnamon

½ tsp. ground cloves
¼ tsp. allspice
¼ tsp. salt
2 tsp. baking powder
1 lb. raisins
1 lb. currants
1 lb. English walnut meats, chopped

Drain the applesauce as dry as possible. Add the soda to it. Cream together thoroughly the sugar and the butter. Add in the applesauce and stir thoroughly.

Sift the flour, then sift it again with the spices, the salt and the baking powder. Blend it into the applesauce mixture. Coat the fruit and the nuts with a little flour and add them into the batter. If there appears to be too much flour, thin to cake batter consistency with a little buttermilk or sour milk.

Bake in a 350° oven in a greased and floured 13 × 9-inch loaf pan for 55 to 60 minutes.

Frost with Brown Sugar Icing, No. 2, (See p. 170).

℞ Rare, Historical and Offbeat Cakes
Chapter 12

APPLE LAYER CAKE

½ cup shortening
2 cups granulated sugar
3 egg yolks
3 cups all-purpose flour,
              sifted

2 tsp. baking powder
¼ tsp. salt
1 cup milk
3 egg whites

Cream the shortening with the sugar in a mixing bowl. Beat the egg yolks well and stir them in. Sift the flour with the baking powder and salt; add into the creamed mixture alternately with the milk. Lastly, beat the egg whites stiffly and fold them in.

Bake in three 8-inch greased and floured layer cake pans at 325° for 30 minutes. Fill the layers with the following special filling.

Special Filling for Apple Layer Cake

1½ cups applesauce
1 cup confectioners sugar
       (more or less according
          to the liquid content
          of the applesauce)

1 tsp. lemon juice
1 tsp. cinnamon

Add the juice and cinnamon to the applesauce in a small bowl; beat in the sugar until the mixture attains a thick custard-like consistency.

TOOTHLESS NELL'S CAKE

(Toothless Nell lies buried in Boot Hill at Dodge City, Kansas. Wyatt Earp, Bat Masterson and other law men of that day probably tried to keep her in bounds. We are told she liked this cake. How she ate it without teeth history doesn't record.)

3 Tbsp. granulated sugar	¼ tsp. cinnamon
¾ stick butter	½ tsp. salt
1 cup dark molasses	1 tsp. baking soda
2 cups all-purpose flour, sifted	1 egg, unbeaten
	4 Tbsp. warm water
¼ tsp. ground cloves	

Cream the sugar and butter together thoroughly. Mix in the molasses. Stir together.

Sift together the flour, spices, salt, and the baking soda.

Break the egg into the sugar and butter mixture and stir it in. Now add in the water gradually and stir it in.

Blend in gradually the sifted flour mix and beat until the batter is quite smooth.

Bake in a 9-inch greased and floured pan for 25 to 30 minutes at 325°. (If desired, when the cake is cool cover it with your favorite icing.)

POTATO FUDGE CAKE

2 sticks butter	½ tsp. salt
2 cups granulated sugar	½ tsp. allspice
4 eggs, separated	½ tsp. cinnamon
1 cup raw potatoes, grated	½ tsp. ground cloves
Grated rind of 1 lemon	½ cup milk
2½ cups all-purpose flour, sifted	3 squares unsweetened chocolate
3 tsp. baking powder	½ cup chopped almonds

Cream the butter; add the sugar gradually and continue blending. Beat the egg yolks well and add them to the creamed mixture along with the grated potato and the lemon rind. Sift the flour once, then measure it. Sift it again with the baking powder, the salt, and the spices.

Add the milk and the sifted dry ingredients alternately to the potato mix. Then melt the chocolate and add it in. Finally, dust the almonds with a little flour and mix them in. Beat the egg whites stiffly and fold them into the batter.

Bake the cake slowly for 1 hour in a 9 × 5-inch greased and floured loaf pan at 325°.

Cover the cake when it is cool with a fluffy white or a chocolate icing.

TOMATO SOUP SPICE CAKE

1 stick butter	½ tsp. cinnamon
1½ cups granulated sugar	½ tsp. ground cloves
2 eggs	1 tsp. baking powder
1 tsp. baking soda	1 can condensed tomato soup
2 Tbsp. water	½ cup nut meats, chopped
2½ cups cake flour, sifted	½ cup raisins
½ tsp. nutmeg	

Cream the butter with the sugar until they are light and fluffy. Beat the eggs well and add them in. Dissolve the soda in the water and stir it into the egg mixture.

Sift 2 cups of flour with the spices and the baking powder. Add this to the mixture alternately with the tomato soup.

Roll the nuts and raisins in the remaining half cup of flour and add them to the batter.

Bake at 350° in a square 9-inch greased and floured pan for one hour.

SALAD DRESSING CAKE

1½ cups granulated sugar	1 tsp. vanilla
1 cup creamy salad dressing	2 tsp. baking soda
2 cups all-purpose flour, sifted	1 cup warm water
3 Tbsp. cocoa	½ tsp. salt

Mix together all the ingredients and beat hard for two minutes.

Bake in an oblong 13 × 9 × 2-inch greased and floured pan at 350° for 30 minutes.

STRAWBERRY POP CAKE

2 cups granulated sugar	1 cup strawberry soda pop
¾ cup shortening	5 egg whites, beaten stiff but not dry
3 cups cake flour, sifted	
2 tsp. baking powder	1 tsp. vanilla
1 tsp. salt	½ tsp. almond extract

Cream the sugar with the shortening.

Sift the flour with the baking powder and salt; add it into the creamed mix, alternately with the soda pop. Fold in the beaten egg whites. Add in the extracts. Stir the total batter gently.

Bake in two greased and floured 9-inch layer cake pans at 350° for 40 minutes.

Frost the cake with Yummy Pale Pink Icing, (See p. 175).

CHOPPED PEANUT CAKE

2 cups cake flour, sifted	⅔ cup milk
1⅓ cups granulated sugar	1 tsp. vanilla
¾ tsp. salt	¼ cup milk (separately)
2½ tsp. baking powder	2 eggs
½ cup shortening, softened	1½ cups shelled raw peanuts

Sift the flour, sugar, salt, and baking powder together in a mixing bowl. Add the shortening; cream together; add in the ⅔ cup of milk and the vanilla. Beat for two minutes, then add the ¼ cup of milk. Beat together again. Add the eggs and beat for two minutes more.

Run the peanuts through a food grinder (or chop them very fine) and then mix them into the batter. Pour the mixture into two deep 8-inch layer cake pans that have been greased and floured. Put pans in a 350° preheated oven and bake for 25 to 30 minutes.

Remove the cake from the pans; allow it to cool; then ice with Peanut Butter Icing, (See p. 174).

(This cake should be allowed to stand about two days before it is eaten, in order to heighten the flavor of the peanuts.)

FIG CAKE

1½ cups granulated sugar
1¼ sticks butter
1 cup milk
3 cups cake flour, sifted
½ tsp. salt
4 tsp. baking powder
4 egg whites, beaten

1 tsp. lemon extract
1 tsp. cinnamon
1 tsp. nutmeg
1½ cups finely cut figs
(10 oz. pkg.)
1 Tbsp. molasses

Cream the sugar with the butter. Add the milk. Sift the flour, salt and baking powder together. Add one-half of the flour mixture to the first ingredients, then add in the well-beaten egg whites. Blend in. Now blend in the rest of the flour and the lemon extract.

To about ⅔ of the mixture add the cinnamon, the nutmeg, the figs (floured lightly first) and the molasses. Using an 8-inch greased and floured round tube pan for the baking, alternately spoon into it the dark and light mixtures, as for marble cake.

Bake at 350° for about 55 minutes.

APPLE JAM CAKE (This Recipe Is over 50 Years Old)

½ stick butter
1 cup granulated sugar
2 eggs
1 cup milk

2 cups all-purpose flour, sifted
¼ tsp. salt
2 tsp. baking powder
1 tsp. vanilla

Cream the butter; add in the sugar gradually. Cream together well. Beat the eggs and add them in. Then add the milk.

Sift together the flour, salt and baking powder. Add these to the creamed mixture and also add the vanilla.

Bake in two greased and floured 9-inch layer cake pans at 375° for about 20 minutes. Set the cake aside to cool and prepare the filling.

Filling

3 large red apples
1 cup granulated sugar

juice of 1 lemon with grated rind

Core the apples, then grate them (the skin as well as the pulp). Add in the juice and lemon rind, then the sugar. Simmer slowly in a saucepan on top of the stove for about 20 minutes, stirring constantly to prevent the mixture from sticking. When it is done it should be a nice clear red color. Cool this filling. When the cake is also cool, spread the filling between the layers and frost the surface of the cake with a white frosting.

DOUBLE BUTTERSCOTCH CAKE

⅔ cup butterscotch morsels	¼ tsp. baking powder
¼ cup water	1¼ cups granulated sugar
2¼ cups cake flour, sifted	1 stick butter
1 tsp. salt	3 eggs
1 tsp. baking soda	1 cup buttermilk or sour milk

Melt the butterscotch morsels with the water in a saucepan; set aside to cool.

Sift the flour with the salt, soda, and baking powder; set aside.

Add the sugar gradually to the butter, creaming well. Blend in the eggs one at a time; beat vigorously after adding each. Now add in the melted butterscotch and mix well. Then add in the dry ingredients alternately with the milk. Beat well.

Turn the batter into two 9-inch layer cake pans, well greased and floured. Bake at 375° for 25 to 35 minutes. Let the cake cool.

Spread Butterscotch Filling, (See p. 158) between layers and on top to within ½ inch of edge of cake. Frost the sides and top edge of the cake with Sea Foam Frosting, (See p. 166), or with whipped cream.

SPUD AND SPICE CAKE

1¾ cups granulated sugar	3 eggs, unbeaten
1 cup cold cooked mashed potatoes	1 tsp. baking soda
	1 cup buttermilk
¾ cup shortening	2 cups plus 2 Tbsp. all-purpose flour, sifted
1 tsp. cinnamon	
½ tsp. nutmeg	¾ cups chopped walnuts
½ tsp. salt	

Combine in a mixing bowl the sugar, potatoes, shortening, spices and salt. Cream for 4 minutes. Add in the eggs; blend well.

Combine the soda and the buttermilk. Add them alternately with 2 cups of flour to the creamed mixture. Coat the nuts with 2 Tbsp. flour; stir them into the batter.

Turn the batter into a greased and floured 13 × 9 × 2-inch pan. Bake at 350° for 50 to 60 minutes. Frost with Quick Caramel Frosting, (See p. 166).

BLACK BEAR'S CAKE*

¾ cup dark molasses
1 stick butter
1 Tbsp. honey
1 egg, well beaten
½ cup warm black coffee

1¾ cups all-purpose flour, sifted
1 tsp. baking soda
½ cup black walnut meats, chopped

Stir together in a mixing bowl the molasses, butter, honey, and the egg. Add in the coffee, then the flour sifted in with the soda. Beat vigorously. Mix in the nuts thoroughly.

Pour the batter into a 9-inch greased and floured tube cake pan and bake in a 350° oven for 50 to 55 minutes.

* *The Story of Black Bear's Cake:* When the American people began moving from the east to the southwest and westward, they went in covered wagons and on horseback. The women sweetened the cakes they made with molasses and honey, as sugar was a rarity. This molasses cake was cooked over campfires and in fireplaces.

By the time, some hundred years later, when this recipe reached our family, it was called Black Bear's Cake. And the recipe came with a legendary tale of how the cake got its name.

A pioneer family living in a log cabin was visited regularly by a shaggy black bear with a crippled foot. When he came to the edge of the clearing begging for food, they would put out their scraps. Often the woman would give him a piece of stale molasses cake. She noticed the bear came quickly the moment the aroma of the cake, baking in the fireplace, filled the air. The husband coming home one day found his wife baking the cake. He cried out, "Oh, you're baking Black Bear's cake!"—L.R. and R.V.

APPLE CIDER CAKE

2½ cups cake flour, sifted   1½ cups granulated sugar
2 tsp. baking powder   ¾ cup shortening
¼ tsp. baking soda   ¾ cup sweet apple cider
1 tsp. salt   3 eggs, unbeaten
1 tsp. cinnamon   Crab apple jelly

Sift together the flour, baking powder, soda, salt, cinnamon and sugar. Place the shortening in a mixing bowl and cream it until it is soft. Sift in the dry ingredients. Add the cider and mix until all the flour is dampened. Beat 2 minutes in a mixer at low speed or by hand for 5 minutes. Add in the eggs and beat one minute more.

Pour the batter into two well greased and floured 8-inch layer cake pans. Bake for 35 to 40 minutes at 350°. When the cake is done, let it cool. Slice the layers in half; spread crab apple jelly over one slice, cover with a second slice; spread lightly with Basic Boiled Icing, (See p. 169), tinted yellow. Repeat until all slices are used. Cover the sides of the cake with the remaining icing.

CHOPPED APPLE CAKE

4 cups chopped tart apples   2 cups all-purpose flour,
1 cup water (from cooked   sifted, plus
            apple peelings)   1 Tbsp. flour
2 cups brown sugar   1 tsp. baking soda
½ cup shortening   ¼ tsp. salt
                                 1 tsp. baking powder

Wash the apples thoroughly; dry them with a soft cloth; peel them. Put the peelings in cold water, bring them to a boil and let them simmer for 10 minutes. Drain off the water and save it; discard the peelings. Chop up the apples.

Cream the sugar with the shortening. Sift in the flour, the soda, salt, and baking powder. Blend thoroughly. Put in the water and stir again. Then add in the chopped apples. Blend together well.

Bake in a 9 × 5-inch greased and floured loaf pan at 350° for about 50 to 55 minutes or until the cake tests done (when a toothpick inserted in the center comes out dry).

SWEET POTATO CAKE

½ cup shortening	¼ tsp. baking soda
1 cup granulated sugar	2 tsp. baking powder
2 eggs	½ tsp. cinnamon
1 cup mashed cooked sweet potatoes	½ tsp. nutmeg
	¼ tsp. ground cloves
2 cups all-purpose flour, sifted	½ cup milk
½ tsp. salt	½ cup chopped nuts

Cream the shortening. Add in the sugar gradually and continue to cream. Add the eggs, one at a time, beating well after each. Add in the sweet potatoes. Mix well. Sift together the flour, salt, soda, baking powder, and the spices. Add them alternately with the milk to the creamed mixture, beginning and ending with the dry ingredients. Add in the nuts. Mix well.

Bake in a greased and floured 9 × 9 × 2-inch square pan in a 350° oven for 45 to 50 minutes. Top with a caramel icing, if desired.

VERA BRANNON'S ORANGE JUICE DATE CAKE

2 sticks butter	1⅓ cups buttermilk
2 cups granulated sugar	1 (10 oz.) pkg. pitted dates, chopped
4 eggs	
4 cups all-purpose flour, sifted	1 cup pecan meats, chopped
1 tsp. salt	2 Tbsp. grated orange rind
1 tsp. baking soda	1 tsp. vanilla

Cream together the butter and the sugar. Beat the eggs and add them in. Then sift the flour, the salt and the soda together and add them in alternately with the buttermilk. Now put in the dates, the nuts, the orange rind, and the vanilla. Combine well together.

Pour the batter into a lightly greased and floured 12-inch tube pan. Bake in a slow oven, 300 to 325°, for 1½ hours, or until the cake is firm to the touch.

While the cake is baking, mix for the topping:

1⅓ cups fresh orange juice	2 cups granulated sugar
1 Tbsp. grated orange rind	

Mix these ingredients well together until the sugar is dissolved. Let the mixture set until the cake is baked.

As soon as the cake is taken from the oven, stir the topping mixture again and pour it over the hot cake in the pan. As you pour slowly, punch holes in the cake with a long-tined fork or a toothpick. The cake will gradually absorb the juice. Let the cake stand in the pan 5 hours or longer.

This recipe makes a large cake but it will keep moist for days. Store it in the refrigerator covered with aluminum foil.

CARROT EGGLESS CAKE

1 cup brown sugar	2 tsp. cinnamon
1¼ cups water	1 tsp. salt
⅓ cup shortening	1 tsp. baking soda
½ cup chopped raisins	2 tsp. water
1 cup grated raw carrots	2 cups all-purpose flour, sifted
½ tsp. nutmeg	2½ tsp. baking powder
½ tsp. ground cloves	½ cup chopped walnut meats

Mix the brown sugar, the water, shortening, raisins, carrots and the spices in a saucepan and boil for 3 minutes. Cool this mixture to lukewarm.

Mix together the salt, the soda, and 2 Tbsp. of water. Add these into the brown sugar mixture.

Sift the flour and the baking powder together and blend them in to the mix. Fold in the nuts.

Bake in a greased and floured 8 $\times$ 4 $\times$ 2½-inch pan at 350° for 1 hour. Frost with Lemon Cream Butter Icing, (See p. 173).

MILKY WAY CAKE

8 Milky Way bars	1½ cups buttermilk
2½ sticks butter	2½ cups cake flour, sifted
2 cups granulated sugar	½ tsp. salt
4 eggs, well beaten	2 tsp. vanilla
½ tsp. baking soda	1 cup chopped nuts

Melt the Milky Way bars in a double boiler with 1 stick of butter. Set the pan aside to cool.

Cream the sugar and the remaining butter together smoothly. Add in the eggs. Then dissolve the soda in the buttermilk and add them in. Sift the flour with the salt and mix it into the batter. Stir thoroughly. Add the vanilla, nuts, and melted bars. Beat everything together well.

Bake the cake in a greased and floured 9-inch tube pan for 1 hour or more at 325°, until it tests done by the toothpick test.

Frost with Chocolate Chip Nut Icing, (See p. 171).

GREEN APPLE CAKE

1 cup brown sugar, packed	1 cup cold coffee
2/3 cup shortening	1 tsp. baking soda in 1/4 cup cold water
2 eggs	
1 cup all-purpose flour, sifted	1/4 cup breakfast cereal bran
1 cup whole wheat flour	1 cup raisins
1/2 tsp. salt	1 cup chopped nuts
2 tsp. pumpkin pie spice	2 green apples, peeled and coarsely chopped

Cream the sugar and the shortening in a large mixing bowl. Beat the eggs and add them to the mixture. Sift together the flours, salt and spice and add them to the batter alternately with the coffee and soda-and-water. Now stir the bran in well.

Dust the raisins and nuts lightly with flour and add them to the batter; then put in the chopped apples. Mix the total batter thoroughly.

Bake as a loaf cake in a greased and floured 11 × 4½-inch pan at 350° for about 50 to 55 minutes.

CRAZY CAKE

1½ cups all-purpose flour, sifted	4 Tbsp. cocoa
1 cup granulated sugar	5 Tbsp. melted shortening
½ tsp. salt	1 Tbsp. vinegar
1 tsp. baking soda	1 tsp. vanilla
1 tsp. baking powder	1 cup water

Measure all the ingredients into a mixing bowl. Beat them together for 2 or 3 minutes. Pour the batter into a greased and floured 9-inch tube pan and bake for 35 to 40 minutes at 350°.

SALT PORK CAKE

2 cups boiling water	1 tsp. baking powder
1 lb. ground salt pork	1 tsp. nutmeg
4 cups granulated sugar	1 tsp. cinnamon
½ cup molasses	1 tsp. ground cloves
1 egg, beaten	1 (15 oz.) pkg. seedless
6 cups all-purpose flour, sifted	raisins

Pour the water over the pork and let it stand until it is lukewarm. Stir in the sugar, the molasses and the egg.

Sift the flour, the baking powder, and the spices together. Add them into the pork mixture. Then flour the raisins lightly and add them in. Mix the total combination thoroughly.

Turn the batter into two greased and floured loaf pans, about 9 × 5 inches, lined with lightly greased wax paper. Bake in a 300° oven for 2 hours.

This recipe makes 2 cakes.

PUMPKIN CAKE

½ cup shortening	4 tsp. baking powder
1 tsp. maple extract	⅛ tsp. salt
1¼ cups brown sugar	1 tsp. cinnamon
2 eggs	¼ tsp. ground cloves
1 cup cooked, strained pumpkin	¼ tsp. allspice
3 cups cake flour, sifted	¼ tsp. nutmeg
¼ tsp. baking soda	¾ cup milk
	1 cup chopped walnuts

Cream the shortening and add in the maple extract. Add in the sugar gradually, creaming constantly until the mixture is light and fluffy.

Beat the eggs until they are light and add them in slowly to the creamed mixture. Continue beating. Now stir in the pumpkin.

Sift together the flour, soda, baking powder, the salt, and the spices, and add them alternately with the milk into the creamed mixture, stirring after each addition. Lastly, fold in the nuts.

Turn the batter into three greased and floured 8-inch layer cake pans lined with lightly greased wax paper. Bake in a moderate oven at 350° for 25 minutes. Ice as desired.

HOT POTATO CAKE

2 cups all-purpose flour, sifted
½ tsp. salt
2 tsp. baking powder
1 tsp. cinnamon
½ tsp. nutmeg
½ tsp. ground cloves
1 stick butter
2 cups granulated sugar
1 cup plain hot mashed potatoes

3 squares unsweetened chocolate, melted
1½ tsp. baking soda
¼ cup water
4 eggs, separated
½ cup milk
½ cup chopped nuts
1 tsp. vanilla

Sift together the flour, the salt, baking powder, and the spices. Set this aside.

Cream the butter with the sugar, then add in the hot mashed potatoes and the melted chocolate. Dissolve the soda in the water and add this into the mix. Beat thoroughly. Then beat the egg yolks and mix them in. Now put in the dry ingredients and the milk alternately. Continue beating. Beat the egg whites; fold them in. Lastly, add the nuts and the vanilla.

Bake in two 9-inch greased and floured layer cake pans at 375° for about 30 to 40 minutes. Ice the cake with either a white or a chocolate icing.

OVERNIGHT CAKE

2 cups granulated sugar
2 cups water
¾ cup shortening, melted
1 cup raisins
1 tsp. cinnamon

1 tsp. ground cloves
1 tsp. nutmeg
2 tsp. baking soda
3 cups all-purpose flour, sifted

Simmer the sugar, water, shortening, raisins, and the spices together in a saucepan for 10 minutes on top of the stove. Let the mixture stand overnight in the pan.

Next morning, simmer for 10 more minutes. Then let the mix cool.

When the mixture is lukewarm, sift the soda into the flour and add them into the cooked mixture. Stir together well.

Bake in an 8 × 4-inch greased and floured loaf pan at 350° for 45 to 50 minutes, or until the cake tests done with the toothpick test.

SCOTCH OATMEAL CAKE

1¾ cups uncooked oatmeal
1½ cups all-purpose flour,
            sifted
1 cup brown sugar
1 tsp. baking soda
½ tsp. salt
¾ cup buttermilk

1¼ sticks butter

For Filling
½ cup chopped nuts
1 lb. dates, chopped
¾ cup water
1 tsp. vanilla

Mix the cake ingredients together thoroughly until they are crumbly.

Cook the date filling ingredients (except the vanilla) in a saucepan on top of the stove over low heat until it thickens. Remove the pan from the fire; add in the vanilla.

Spread one-half of the cake mixture in a 9-inch square pan, that has been greased and floured. Add a layer of date filling and top with the remaining batter. Bake at 350° for about 35 minutes. Cut the cake into squares while it is warm but serve it cold.

EMMA STEPHENSON'S FRESH COCONUT CAKE

1 stick butter or margarine
1½ cups granulated sugar
1 tsp. vanilla
2 cups cake flour, sifted
2 tsp. baking powder
¼ tsp. baking soda
½ tsp. salt

½ cup buttermilk
1 medium-sized coconut
           to yield
½ cup coconut milk
1¼ cups grated fresh coco-
           nut meat
4 egg whites, stiffly beaten

(*To prepare the fresh coconut:* Pierce the eyes of the coconut with an ice pick. Drain off the milk into a clean container. Crack the shell all over with heavy blows of a hammer or mallet. Remove the outer shell and pare off the dark inner skin. Grate the white meat—leftover pieces can be wrapped in foil and stored in the refrigerator for later use.)

Cream the butter until it is fluffy. Add the sugar in 4 parts, creaming after each addition. Add in the vanilla. Sift the flour, the baking powder, the soda, and the salt together and add them alternately to the creamed mixture with the buttermilk and the coconut milk. Add in ¼ cup of the grated coconut. Then fold in the egg whites, gently but thoroughly. Pour the batter into two greased and floured 8-inch layer cake pans.

Bake in a 350° oven for 35 minutes. Cool the layers on a cake rack and then frost them with Butter Frosting (See p. 160). After the cake is frosted, sprinkle all over it generously with the remaining cup of grated fresh coconut meat.

ICEBOX GINGER CAKE

2 sticks butter	2 tsp. ginger
1 cup granulated sugar	¼ tsp. cinnamon
4 eggs	¼ tsp. allspice
1 cup molasses	¼ tsp. salt
2 tsp. baking soda	½ cup raisins
1 cup buttermilk	½ cup chopped nut meats
4 cups all-purpose flour	

Cream the butter with the sugar. Add the eggs, one at a time, beating well after each addition. Add in the molasses and beat well. Stir the soda into the milk and add them into the mixture.

Sift the flour with the spices and the salt. Then add it into the batter. Dust the raisins and nuts lightly with flour and fold them in gently.

Put the batter in a covered bowl and place it in the refrigerator. This batter will keep for a month and can be baked in muffin pans as needed. To bake, bring the batter to room temperature, pour lightly greased and floured muffin tins ¾ full, and bake in a 350° oven for 20 to 25 minutes.

WACKY CAKE

1 tsp. baking soda	⅓ cup cocoa
1 cup water	1 tsp. vanilla
1½ cups all-purpose flour, sifted	1 tsp. vinegar
1 cup granulated sugar	½ cup melted butter or cooking oil

Dissolve the soda in the water. Sift the flour, sugar and cocoa together into an 8-inch square pan. Make 3 holes in the mixture.

Into the first hole pour the vanilla and the vinegar.

Into the second hole put the soda-water.

Into the third hole pour the melted butter or oil.

Beat for 1 minute at medium speed.

Bake in the same pan for 30 minutes at 350°.

OLDFASHIONED LEMON CAKE

1 stick butter
1½ cups granulated sugar
4 eggs, separated
1 tsp. lemon extract
½ tsp. grated lemon rind

4½ cups cake flour, sifted
2 tsp. baking powder
¼ tsp. salt
¾ cup milk

Cream the butter and sugar together until they are creamy.

Separate the yolks from the whites of the eggs and beat each separately. Beat the egg yolks until they are pale and thick and add them into the creamed mixture. Add in the lemon extract and the rind, and then add the dry ingredients alternately with the milk. Lastly, fold in the stiffly beaten egg whites.

Bake in two greased and floured 9-inch layer cake pans in a 375° oven for 20 to 30 minutes. Put the layers together with a lemon filling.

CAMPFIRE CAKE

2 sticks butter
1 cup granulated sugar
4 eggs, unbeaten
1 tsp. vanilla

¼ cup milk or ¾ Tbsp. powdered milk
2 cups all-purpose flour
1 tsp. baking powder
1 tsp. salt

Mix all the ingredients in the pan in which you will cook it. Any shallow pan or aluminum skillet will do. Melt the butter before adding it in.

Stir the batter with a fork in a circular motion for 10 minutes.

Bake in any kind of a camp or covered oven for 1 hour, and don't let it smoke. If the oven smokes, it is too near the fire.

Serves 10.

ROSY APPLESAUCE CAKE

1 cup granulated sugar
½ cup shortening, softened
2 Tbsp. unsweetened pine-
      apple juice
¾ cup unsweetened apple-
      sauce
1 tsp. red food coloring

2 cups all-purpose flour,
      sifted
1½ tsp. baking powder
¼ tsp. salt
1 tsp. baking soda
1 egg, well beaten
½ cup milk
½ cup shredded coconut

Cream together the sugar and the shortening. Add the pineapple juice and stir it in. Stir in the applesauce and the coloring.

Sift the flour, measure it, and sift it again with the baking powder, the salt, and the soda. Add the egg to the batter; then blend in the flour mixture alternately with the milk. Last of all, fold in the coconut. Beat for about 30 seconds by hand.

Bake in a 9-inch tube pan for 35 minutes at 325–350°. When the cake is cool, cover it with Snow Peak Icing, (See page 175), and spread shredded coconut generously over the top.

❧ Transforming Commercial Mixes

Chapter 13

LEMON GELATIN CAKE

1 pkg. white cake mix	4 whole eggs
1 pkg. lemon gelatin powder	1 tsp. lemon extract
¾ cup cooking oil	1½ cups confectioners sugar
¾ cup water	6 Tbsp. fresh lemon juice

Mix the cake mix directly from the package with the gelatin powder, the cooking oil and the water. Add the eggs, one at a time, and beat after each. Add in the lemon extract.

Pour the mixture into a greased and floured 13 × 9-inch oblong pan. Bake at 350° for from 30 to 40 minutes. While the cake is baking mix the confectioners sugar with the lemon juice.

When the cake is done, remove it from the oven and immediately poke holes in it with a toothpick while slowly pouring the sugar-lemon juice combination over the cake. The hot cake will soon absorb this topping.

Cover the pan with aluminum foil and when it has cooled set it in the refrigerator for 24 hours before cutting it into squares and serving it.

This cake may be served right from the pan (a glass baking pan is ideal for this cake).

PRUNE COFFEE CAKE

½ stick butter, melted
¼ cup brown sugar, packed
3 Tbsp. corn syrup
1 egg, beaten
½ cup pitted, cooked prunes,
                   cut up
½ cup liquid from cooked
                 prunes

2½ cups packaged dry bis-
                  cuit mix
½ tsp. cinnamon
⅓ cup granulated sugar
½ cup chopped walnuts
9 whole cooked prunes,
                 pitted

Into the melted butter stir the brown sugar and the corn syrup. Set this aside.

Combine the egg, half a cup of cut prunes, the prune liquid, the biscuit mix, the cinnamon and the white sugar. Stir until blended.

Spread the mixture in a 9-inch square greased and floured pan. Sprinkle on the walnuts and arrange the whole prunes on top. Spoon the brown sugar mixture over all.

Bake in a hot oven at 400° for 30 minutes. Serve warm.

LEMON GINGERBREAD CAKE

½ stick butter
½ cup brown sugar

1 lemon
1 pkg. gingerbread mix

Melt the butter in a 9-inch square cake pan. Blend in the brown sugar until it is melted and smooth. Spread evenly in the pan. Cut the lemon into nine very thin slices, then quarter them. Arrange the lemon sections evenly over the sugar-butter in the pan.

Prepare the gingerbread mix according to directions on the package. Pour the batter very carefully over the lemon slices.

Bake at 350° for 30 minutes. When the cake is done, invert the pan on a serving plate.

CHERRY DREAM CAKE

1 lb. frozen cherries, thawed
   and drained. (Save the juice)
⅓ cup granulated sugar
¼ tsp. salt
¼ tsp. almond flavoring

3 Tbsp. cornstarch
1 small pkg. white cake mix
2 cups heavy cream
2 Tbsp. granulated sugar
½ tsp. vanilla

Cook the cherries, the sugar, salt, and the almond flavoring in a saucepan until they come to a boil. Put the cherry juice and the cornstarch in a shaker and mix them well; then add this liquid to the cherries and cook until the mixture is very thick. As this cooks, mix the cake as directed on the package.

Grease and lightly flour a 2-quart casserole with butter; place the cherry mixture in the casserole; pour the cake batter over it, covering all the cherries. Do not stir.

Bake at 350° for 35 to 40 minutes. When done, invert the pan onto a cake plate that has an upturned edge. Some of the cherries will fall but can be replaced when the cake has cooled.

After the cake has cooled, whip the cream and flavor it with the 2 Tbsp. sugar and the vanilla. Frost the cake with the whipped cream. (A few uncooked cherries may be withheld to garnish.)

LEMON SPECIAL CAKE

1 box lemon cake mix
        (1 lb. 3½ oz.)
½ cup granulated sugar
¾ cup cooking oil
¼ tsp. salt

1 cup apricot nectar
4 eggs
2 cups confectioners sugar
Juice of 2 lemons

Combine the cake mix, the granulated sugar, the oil, the salt and the apricot nectar together. Add the eggs, one at a time. Mix well.

Bake in a 13 × 9 × 2-inch greased and floured pan for 30 to 35 minutes at 325°. When the cake is still warm, pour the following glaze over it.

Glaze: Mix the confectioners sugar with the lemon juice.

RAISIN COFFEE CAKE

1 cup golden seedless raisins	1 egg
2⅓ cups packaged biscuit mix powder	⅔ cup milk
	¼ stick butter, melted
⅓ cup granulated sugar	

For Topping

⅓ cup biscuit mix powder	¼ stick butter
3 Tbsp. granulated sugar	

Combine the raisins, the biscuit mix, and the sugar. Beat the egg lightly and combine it with the milk and the melted butter. Add the egg mix into the dry mixture, blending in well. Turn the batter into a greased and floured 9-inch square pan.

Blend the topping ingredients until they are crumbly and sprinkle them over the batter.

Bake in a moderately hot oven at 375° for 30 to 40 minutes. This cake should be served warm.

LEMON POUND CAKE

1 pkg. lemon cake mix (or any yellow cake mix)	⅔ cup cooking oil
	4 eggs
1 pkg. lemon gelatin powder	Grated rind of 1 lemon
⅔ cup cold water	

Put together all the ingredients, except the rind, and beat thoroughly in a mixer or by hand. Then add in the rind.

Pour into a greased and floured 13 × 9 × 2-inch pan and bake at 350° for from 45 minutes to 1 hour.

EASY-DOES-IT CAKE

1 pkg. white cake mix	2 eggs, unbeaten
1 pkg. chocolate pudding mix	2 cups milk

Mix all the ingredients together thoroughly. Bake in two 9-inch greased and floured round pans for 40 to 45 minutes at 350°. Frost with a favorite icing.

To vary this recipe try a lemon pudding mix instead of the chocolate pudding.

DATE BAR FRUIT CAKE

1 pkg. date bar mix	1 tsp. cinnamon
⅔ cup hot water	¼ tsp. nutmeg
3 eggs	¼ tsp. allspice
¼ cup all-purpose flour	1 cup chopped nuts
½ tsp. salt	1 cup candied fruit, chopped
¾ tsp. baking powder	1 cup raisins
2 Tbsp. light molasses	

Heat the oven to 325°. Grease and flour a 9 × 5 × 3-inch loaf pan.

Combine the envelope of date filling from the mix package with the hot water in a large bowl. Add to this the crumbly mix from the package, the eggs, flour, salt, baking powder, molasses and spices. Blend well. Dust the nuts and fruit very lightly with flour and fold them in thoroughly. Pour the batter into the prepared pan.

Bake about 1 hour and 20 minutes, or until the cake tests done when probed with a toothpick. Cool the cake thoroughly. Wrap it tightly in wax paper and refrigerate it.

ANGEL DELIGHT CAKE

One angel food cake (made from a mix, if desired) cut into three equal layers.

Combine in a large mixing bowl:

1 pkg. frozen strawberries, thawed	1 egg white
¾ cup granulated sugar	1 tsp. lemon juice

Beat these four ingredients 5 to 10 minutes with an electric beater at high speed or with a hand beater vigorously for 12 minutes.

Ice between the layers and on top and sides of the cake with the strawberry mix.

EASY CHEESE CAKE

1 pkg. frozen slice-and-bake sugar cookies	2 eggs, beaten 1 stick butter or margarine
1½ lbs. cream cheese	¼ tsp. salt
1 cup granulated sugar	1 tsp. vanilla

Line 2 greased and floured 8-inch round pans with slices of the frozen sugar cookies.

Blend the cheese with the sugar thoroughly. Add in the beaten eggs, the softened butter or margarine, the salt, and the vanilla, blending all thoroughly. Pour half of the mixture into each pan.

Bake for 25 minutes in a 400° preheated oven. Garnish with fresh strawberries or other fruit. Each cake serves 8.

STRAWBERRY SPECIAL CAKE

1 pkg. white cake mix (one that calls for no eggs)	½ cup water ½ cup cooking oil
1 pkg. strawberry gelatin powder	½ pkg. frozen strawberries, thawed
3 Tbsp. all-purpose flour	3 eggs

Beat together all the ingredients, except the eggs.

Add in one egg at a time and beat after each addition.

Bake at 350° in three 8-inch greased and floured layer cake pans until the cake is firm when touched lightly (about 30 minutes).

Ice this cake with Frozen Strawberry Icing, (See p. 173).

EASY APPLE GINGER CAKE

¼ stick butter	2 Tbsp. grated orange rind
4 cups tart apples, peeled and sliced	2 Tbsp. orange juice 1 pkg. gingerbread mix
1 cup granulated sugar	

Melt the butter in a 9-inch square baking pan. Arrange apple slices on the butter and sprinkle the sugar and orange rind over them. Dribble the orange juice over the apples and the rind and simmer in pan on top of the stove over low heat for 5 minutes.

Prepare the gingerbread batter as directed on the package; pour it evenly over the apple mix.

Bake at 350° for 30 minutes, or until the cake begins to shrink from sides of pan. Cool cake 5 minutes. Remove from pan and invert onto plate.

Serve with sweetened whipped cream.

BISCUIT COFFEE CAKE

2 cans refrigerator (not frozen) biscuits	¾ cup (packaged) cinnamon-sugar mixture
½ stick butter, melted	Raisins and nuts

Grease lightly and flour a ring mold or small tube-type pan.

Dip the biscuit slices in the melted butter and then in the cinnamon-sugar mix. Place one layer of the biscuits in the pan and sprinkle on nuts and raisins. Place a second layer of biscuits over the first and sprinkle on a few more raisins and nuts.

Bake in a 400° oven for 15 minutes, or until the cake is browned and the biscuits are done.

Serves 6.

℞ Fillings, Frostings, Icings, Toppings
Chapter 14

HOW TO FROST A CAKE

Painstaking care puts the artistic touch on a homemade cake—use artistry in frosting a cake.

To frost a cake is surprisingly easy. The rules to follow are:

Be sure the cake is cool. Brush off any crumbs.

To frost a two-layer cake: put one layer top side down on a plate. Heap about one-fourth of the frosting in the center of the layer and spread it evenly with a spatula or a knife almost to the cake's edge. Cover this with the second layer, keeping the top side up. Spread frosting on the sides of the cake. Put the balance of the frosting on top of the cake and spread it until the whole is evenly covered.

To frost an oblong cake: put the cake top side up on a cake plate or pan. Spread the frosting with a knife or spatula on the sides of the cake first; then heap the remaining frosting on top of the cake and spread it evenly all over.

You may then decorate either cake with nuts, sprinkles, candy pieces, or with a design in frosting drawn with a pastry tube.

BUTTERSCOTCH FILLING

½ cup granulated sugar
1 Tbsp. cornstarch
½ cup evaporated milk
⅓ cup water
⅓ cup butterscotch morsels
      (crushed)

1 egg yolk, beaten
¼ stick butter
1 cup shredded, chopped
      coconut
1 cup pecan or walnut meats,
      chopped

Put the sugar and cornstarch in a saucepan; stir in the milk, then the water, butterscotch morsels and the egg yolk. Cook over medium heat, stirring constantly until the mixture thickens. Remove the pan from the heat, add in the butter, coconut and nut meats. Blend well. Set the pan aside to cool before the filling is used.

EGG YOLK FILLING

4 egg yolks
¾ cup granulated sugar
2½ Tbsp. cornstarch

¼ tsp. salt
1½ cups milk, scalded
1 tsp. vanilla

Beat the egg yolks; gradually add in the sugar, cornstarch and salt. Pour the scalded milk over this mixture. Cook in a double boiler over boiling water, stirring constantly until the filling has thickened. When it is cool, add in the vanilla, or any other preferred flavoring.

LEMON FILLING

1 cup granulated sugar
3 Tbsp. cornstarch
2 eggs
1 cup water

Juice of 2 large lemons
Grated rind of 1 lemon
¼ stick butter, melted

Mix thoroughly the sugar with the cornstarch. Beat the eggs with a rotary beater and stir them into the water. Add the lemon juice and the rind into the eggs-and-water. Now combine in the sugar mix.

Soften the butter in the top of a double boiler. Combine in the original mixture and stir to mix thoroughly. Place the pan over boiling water and, stirring constantly, cook the mixture until the filling is thick and smooth. Cool to lukewarm before spreading the filling on cake.

LEMON CUSTARD FILLING

1 cup granulated sugar	**1 Tbsp. all-purpose flour**
⅛ stick butter	**1 cup milk**
5 egg yolks	**Grated rind and juice of 2 lemons**

Cream together the sugar and butter. Add in the egg yolks and the flour, blending thoroughly. Then add in the milk. Stir the mixture. Now add the grated rind and the lemon juice. Cook in a double boiler over boiling water, stirring occasionally until the filling is thick enough to spread on the cake as thickly as you wish.

PEANUT BRITTLE FILLING

1 cup peanut brittle   **1 cup heavy cream**

Whip the cream until it is stiff. Run the peanut brittle through a food chopper or roll it by hand until it is thoroughly crumbled. Fold the brittle into the whipped cream and spread the mixture between cake layers. If desired, this filling can also be used as a topping.

PINEAPPLE EGG YOLK FILLING

1 cup granulated sugar	**¼ cup milk**
¼ stick butter	**1 egg yolk, well beaten**
½ tsp. salt	**2 Tbsp. unsweetened pineapple juice**
¼ tsp. grated lemon peel	

Measure all the ingredients, except the pineapple juice, into a saucepan. Stir them together thoroughly. Put the pan on top of the stove and cook over a low flame until the mixture when tested in cold water will form a soft ball.

Stir in the pineapple juice and cook about one-half minute longer. Remove the pan from the stove and beat the mixture until it is smooth.

PRUNE NUT FILLING

1 egg, beaten
½ cup granulated sugar
½ cup milk

½ cup chopped prunes
½ cup chopped nuts

Boil together the egg, the sugar, the milk, and the prunes until the mixture is thick enough to spread, stirring frequently to avoid sticking. Allow the mixture to cool to lukewarm; then add in the nuts.
Spread between the layers and on top of the cake.

RAISIN FILLING

1 cup granulated sugar
4 Tbsp. water

1 cup raisins
1 egg white, well beaten

Boil the water and sugar until they spin a thread. Add the raisins and pour the mix slowly over the beaten egg white. Mix gently.
Spread on the cake and between the layers.

BUTTER FROSTING

¾ cup milk
3½ Tbsp. all-purpose flour
¾ cup granulated sugar

1 stick butter
½ tsp. vanilla
½ tsp. salt

Cook the milk and flour in a saucepan until the mixture thickens. It should look like a paste. Then when this has cooled add in the other ingredients. Beat until they are foamy. (If desired, any other flavoring may be substituted for the vanilla.)

CANDY MOUNTAIN FROSTING

¾ cup granulated sugar
6 Tbsp. white corn syrup
3 Tbsp. water

3 egg whites
½ cup chopped nuts

Mix the sugar, corn syrup and water together thoroughly in a saucepan. Then boil them rapidly on top of the stove until the mixture spins a long thread. Beat the egg whites to stand up in very stiff peaks. Pour the cooked syrup mix slowly over the egg whites, stirring rapidly as you do so. Add in a few drops of red food coloring and any desired flavoring, either almond, vanilla, pineapple, mint or clove. Fold the total mixture together gently.

Decorate the frosted cake with the chopped nuts.

CARAMEL FROSTING

2 egg whites	5 Tbsp. water
1½ cups brown sugar	½ tsp. maple flavoring
Pinch of salt	

Combine all the ingredients, except the flavoring, in the top of a double boiler. Beat 1 minute with a rotary mixer. Place the pan over boiling water; beat constantly until the frosting peaks. Remove the pan from the fire. Add the maple flavoring and beat about 2 minutes longer.

CARROT FROSTING

1 Tbsp. light molasses	1 tsp. vanilla
1 cup granulated sugar	½ tsp. cinnamon
⅛ stick butter, melted	½ cup grated raw carrots
¼ cup milk	

Cook the first four ingredients together until the mixture forms a solid ball when tested in cold water.

Remove the pan from the fire; stir the mixture until its texture becomes grainy. Then add in the vanilla, the cinnamon, and the carrots.

COCOA FROSTING

Using the Creamy Smooth Icing recipe, (See p. 172) add 3 tablespoons of cocoa to the sugar and sift together.

Combine the egg whites, granulated sugar, salt, water, and the syrup in the top of a double boiler. Mix thoroughly with a beater over boiling water.

Add in the vanilla and the powdered sugar and continue beating until the frosting is thick enough for spreading.

Frost the cake on top and between its layers. Then dust all over the cake heavily with the coconut.

COCONUT FROSTING

2 egg whites	2 tsp. corn syrup
1½ cups granulated sugar	1½ tsp. vanilla
¼ tsp. salt	1½ Tbsp. confectioners sugar
⅓ cup water	1 (7 oz.) box shredded coconut

COCONUT PECAN FROSTING

1 cup evaporated milk	1 tsp. vanilla
1 cup granulated sugar	1 can tender, flaked coconut
½ stick margarine	1 cup chopped pecan meats
3 egg yolks	

Combine the milk, sugar and margarine in a saucepan. Add the egg yolks and the vanilla. Cook over medium heat until the mixture thickens (about 12 minutes). Stir it constantly. Remove the pan from the heat; add the coconut and the chopped nuts. Beat the frosting until it is cool and thick enough to spread. (Do not frost the sides of the cake when using this frosting.)

CREAM CHEESE FROSTING

1 3-oz. pkg. cream cheese	2½ cups confectioners sugar, sifted
1 Tbsp. milk	½ tsp. vanilla

Soften the cheese with the milk. Gradually blend in the sugar. Add the vanilla. Mix well until the frosting is smooth.

FUDGE FROSTING

2 squares unsweetened
                  chocolate
2 cups granulated sugar
2 Tbsp. corn syrup

⅔ cup milk
¼ stick butter
1 tsp. vanilla

Cut the chocolate into small pieces. Then cook the sugar, the chocolate, the corn syrup, and the milk together. Stir constantly until the sugar is dissolved. Then stir the mixture occasionally to prevent it burning. Cook until the syrup forms a soft ball when tested in cold water.

Remove the pan from the fire. Add in the butter and cool the mixture to lukewarm. Add in the vanilla and beat steadily until the frosting is creamy and of the right consistency for spreading.

HONEY FROSTING

¼ stick butter
2 Tbsp. honey
2⅓ cups confectioners sugar

Pinch of salt
1 egg white, unbeaten

Cream the butter and the honey together, then add in ⅓ cup of sugar and the salt. Cream again.

Add the egg white alternately with the balance of the sugar, beating well as you add them. When the mixture is smooth, it is ready for use.

HULA FROSTING

2 egg whites, unbeaten
5 Tbsp. pineapple syrup
              (from the can)
1½ cups granulated sugar
⅛ tsp. salt

1 tsp. light corn syrup
½ tsp. vanilla
½ tsp. orange extract
½ cup crushed pineapple,
                  drained

Mix the egg whites, the pineapple syrup, the sugar, the salt, and the corn syrup together thoroughly in a double boiler. Set the pan over boiling water and beat the mixture constantly with a rotary beater until it will hold a peak.

Remove the pan from the hot water and add in the vanilla and the orange extract. Beat again. Then let the mixture cool. When it is cold, fold in the pineapple.

Frost the top and between the layers of the cake.

MAPLE FROSTING

1 cup maple sugar	**⅛ tsp. cream of tartar**
½ cup boiling water	**1 egg white, beaten**

Boil the sugar, water and cream of tartar together until they spin a thread from a spoon. Pour this blend slowly in a stream on the beaten egg white and continue beating until the frosting is thick enough to spread on a cake. (If desired, add a cup of chopped English walnut meats to this frosting.)

MOCHA FROSTING

⅔ cup granulated sugar	**3 Tbsp. strong coffee**
½ cup light corn syrup	**⅛ tsp. salt**
2 egg whites	**1 tsp. vanilla**
1 cup chocolate chips	

Combine the above ingredients, except the vanilla, in a double boiler over rapidly boiling water. Beat with a rotary beater for about 7 or 8 minutes, or until the frosting holds its shape. Remove the pan from the boiling water. Add in the vanilla. Let the frosting cool before spreading it on cooled cake layers. Dot the top of the cake generously with extra chips before the frosting has hardened.

NOUGAT FROSTING

1 egg white, unbeaten	**¼ tsp. cream of tartar**
1 Tbsp. water	**Pinch of salt**
1 Tbsp. honey	**¼ tsp. vanilla**
½ cup granulated sugar	**⅓ cup chopped, blanched and toasted almonds**

Put the above ingredients, except the almonds and the vanilla, in a double boiler and mix them well. Place over rapidly boiling water and beat constantly with a rotary beater until the mixture holds a peak. Remove the pan from the fire, add in the vanilla and the almonds. Then beat until the frosting is of the right consistency to spread over a cake.

NUTMEAT COCONUT FROSTING

½ stick butter	½ cup chopped nutmeats
½ cup brown sugar	¾ cup flaked or shredded
3 Tbsp. half and half cream	coconut

Combine the above ingredients. Blend well. Spread the mixture evenly over the top of the cake.

Place the cake under the broiler (set for low heat) until the frosting becomes bubbly. Serve immediately.

ORANGE FROSTING

Use the Creamy Smooth Icing recipe (p. 172) but omit the vanilla and the cream. Substitute 1 Tbsp. grated orange peel and 2 Tbsp. orange juice.

ORANGE COCONUT FROSTING

3 Tbsp. butter	¼ cup orange juice
2 cups confectioners sugar	¾ cup grated coconut

Cream the butter until it is very smooth. Add the sugar gradually, alternating with a little of the orange juice occasionally, until all the sugar and juice have been creamed in.

Beat the frosting until it is smooth. Then gently beat in the coconut.

ORANGE CREAM FROSTING

1 stick butter	½ cup orange juice
4 Tbsp. cake flour	3 cups confectioners sugar
½ tsp. salt	1 Tbsp. grated orange rind

Melt the butter in a saucepan. Remove the pan from the heat. Blend in the flour and the salt slowly. Stir in the orange juice. Place the pan back over the heat; bring it to a boil, stirring constantly. Again remove the pan from the heat.

Now stir in the powdered sugar and the orange rind. Place the saucepan in a pan of cold water and beat the mixture until it is of a spreading consistency. Add more powdered sugar if necessary.

ORNAMENTAL FROSTING

2 egg whites	1 tsp. lemon juice
1 cup confectioners sugar	Few drops of coloring, if desired

Beat the egg whites until they are frothy, but not stiff. Measure and sift the powdered sugar; sprinkle 2 tsp. over the egg whites and whip them about 5 minutes with a wire whisk. Continue beating in sugar, adding a little at a time, until you have exhausted the cup of sugar. Add in the lemon juice and beat until the frosting will stand up in peaks.

(*Note:* This frosting can be used in a pastry tube to decorate cakes that have already been carefully iced.)

QUICK CARAMEL FROSTING

½ stick butter	3 Tbsp. milk
¾ cup brown sugar	2 cups confectioners sugar

Melt the butter in a saucepan; stir in the brown sugar. Cook over low heat for 2 minutes, stirring frequently. Add in the milk. Bring the mixture to a full boil, take it off the heat, and let it cool to lukewarm.

Then add the confectioners sugar and beat the mixture until the frosting is of spreading consistency.

SEA FOAM FROSTING

⅓ cup granulated sugar	1 Tbsp. corn syrup
⅓ cup brown sugar	1 egg white
⅓ cup water	¼ tsp. cream of tartar

In a saucepan slowly cook together the first four ingredients until the mixture forms a soft ball in cold water.

Beat the egg white with the cream of tartar until they are stiff.

Add the cooked syrup mixture to the egg white, beating constantly. Continue beating until the frosting is thick enough to spread.

SNOW WHITE FROSTING

2 egg whites	Pinch of salt
1½ cups granulated sugar	⅓ cup cold water
1½ tsp. light corn syrup	1 tsp. vanilla

Combine the egg whites, the sugar, the syrup, the salt and the water in the top of a double boiler. Beat for 1 minute with an electric or rotary beater. Place the pan over boiling water and beat constantly until the frosting forms peaks (7–8 minutes). Remove the pan from the boiling water. Add in the vanilla and beat the frosting until it is of a spreading consistency (about 2 minutes).

Frosts the top and sides of two 9-inch layer cakes or one 10-inch tube cake.

(For a smaller quantity of frosting, use half the ingredients and cook about 4 minutes.)

STRAWBERRY FROSTING

2 eggs whites, unbeaten	⅔ cup frozen strawberries, thawed and drained
1 cup granulated sugar	Pinch of salt

Combine all the ingredients in the top of a double boiler. Beat for 1 minute with an electric mixer or rotary beater. Place the pan over boiling water; beat the mixture constantly until the frosting forms peaks. Remove the pan from the boiling water. (Pour the mix into a mixing bowl, if you wish.) Beat the frosting until it is of a spreading consistency (about 2 minutes).

Spread the frosting on the cake and garnish the top with whole strawberries.

SUGARLESS ORANGE FROSTING

2 egg whites	2 Tbsp. orange juice
1½ cups light corn syrup	½ tsp. grated orange peel
⅛ tsp. salt	

Combine the unbeaten egg whites, the corn syrup, and the salt in the top of a double boiler and beat with a rotary beater until they are well mixed. Set the pan over rapidly boiling water and beat continually while the mixture cooks. Cook for seven minutes, or until the frosting will stand in peaks. Remove the pan from the boiling water. Add in the orange juice and the peel and beat until the frosting is thick enough to spread.

SURPRISE FROSTING

¾ stick butter, softened	2 Tbsp. cocoa
3 cups confectioners sugar	1 tsp. cinnamon
½ cup nut meats, chopped	2 Tbsp. hot coffee
2 Tbsp. light cream	

Place all the ingredients in a bowl and mix well until the frosting is very creamy and smooth. Spread the frosting on the cake and decorate it with a few extra nut meats.

VANILLA MARSHMALLOW FROSTING

2 egg whites	¼ cup water
1½ cups granulated sugar	1½ tsp. pure vanilla extract
⅛ tsp. salt	12 marshmallows (regular size)
1 Tbsp. light corn syrup	

Combine the first 5 ingredients in the top of a double boiler. Set the pan over rapidly boiling water. Beat the mix with a rotary beater at full speed for 7 minutes, or until the frosting stands in stiff peaks. Remove the pan from the range and put in the vanilla.

Cut the marshmallows into small pieces. Add them in and beat until the marshmallows have melted.

Spread the frosting between the cake layers and over the top and sides of cake.

BASIC BOILED ICING

2 egg whites, unbeaten	**2 tsp. light corn syrup**
1½ cups granulated sugar	**1 tsp. vanilla**
¼ tsp. salt	**½ tsp. almond extract**
⅓ cup water	

Combine the egg whites, sugar, salt, water, and the corn syrup in the top of a double boiler. Beat for about 1 minute, or until the ingredients are thoroughly mixed. Then place the pan over boiling water and beat constantly with a sturdy rotary beater, or at high speed of an electric beater, for 7 minutes.

Remove the pan from the boiling water, and pour the mixture at once into a large bowl. Add the extracts and beat again until the icing is thick enough to spread.

Makes 4½ cups of frosting, enough to cover a large cake.

BROILED ICING

6 Tbsp. butter or margarine	**½ cup chopped pecan or**
¾ cup brown sugar	**walnut meats**
¾ Tbsp. heavy cream or	**½ cup shredded coconut**
condensed milk	

Melt the butter in a saucepan; mix in the remainder of the ingredients. Blend them together smoothly. Spread over the top of a warm cake.

Place the cake about 3 inches below the broiler coils (set for low heat) and broil until the mixture bubbles and browns.

Serve the cake while the icing is still warm.

BROWN SUGAR ICING, NO. 1

1 stick butter	**¼ cup milk**
1 cup brown sugar	**(Enough powdered sugar to**
	make the right consistency)

Melt the butter and the brown sugar in a pan and bring to a boil. Add in the milk and boil for two minutes, stirring frequently. Set the pan off the stove and cool the mixture. Beat in the powdered sugar, enough to make the right consistency for spreading. (This is one of the easiest to make icings.)

BROWN SUGAR ICING, NO. 2

¾ stick butter	½ cup light cream
2 cups brown sugar	1 cup confectioners sugar

Place the butter, brown sugar and cream in a saucepan. Set on stove over a low flame. Stir occasionally. When the mixture reaches a rolling boil, remove the pan from the heat.

Add in the powdered sugar and beat well until the icing is creamy.

BURNT SUGAR ICING

3 or 4 Tbsp. burnt sugar mixture, made from 1 cup granulated sugar (as directed)	¼ cup shortening
	1 tsp. vanilla
	About 2 Tbsp. cream
2 cups confectioners sugar, sifted	

To make burnt sugar mixture melt 1 cup of sugar in a heavy skillet over low heat until it is medium brown; stir constantly. Remove the skillet from the heat and stir in ½ cup of boiling water. Mix well; if any lumps remain, return the skillet to the heat and melt them. Cool the mixture before using.

Cream together the confectioners sugar, and the shortening; stir in the burnt sugar mixture. Add in the vanilla, and stir in the cream. Beat until the mixture is of spreading consistency.

BUTTERMILK ICING

1 cup granulated sugar	½ tsp. baking soda
½ cup buttermilk	Few drops vanilla
½ stick margarine	

Cook the first four ingredients until a soft ball forms when dropped in cold water. Remove from heat. Add the vanilla and beat until the icing is creamy.

CHOCOLATE ICING

2 squares unsweetened chocolate	1 cup confectioners sugar
¼ stick butter	Pinch of salt
2 Tbsp. hot water	¼ tsp. vanilla

Melt the chocolate in the top of a double boiler. Remove the pan from the hot water. Stir in the butter and 2 Tbsp. of hot water. Blend in the sugar. Beat with a spoon until the mixture is smooth. Then add in the salt and the vanilla.

CHOCOLATE BUTTER ICING

⅓ cup soft butter (about ⅝ stick)	3 Tbsp. heavy cream (scant)
3 cups sifted confectioners sugar	1½ tsp. vanilla
	3 squares (3 oz.) unsweetened chocolate, melted and cooled

Blend the butter with the sugar. Add in the cream and the vanilla. Stir until the mix is smooth. Blend in the melted chocolate. (For extra richness add 1 egg yolk.)

CHOCOLATE CHIP NUT ICING

2 cups granulated sugar	1 (6 oz.) pkg. chocolate chips
1 stick butter	½ cup chopped nuts
1 (13 oz.) can evaporated milk	

Cook the sugar with the butter and the milk until they reach the soft ball stage. (To test, drop a few drops of the mixture into a cup of cold water and roll them between the thumb and first finger.)

Add the chocolate chips and beat until the icing reaches a consistency for spreading. Just before icing the cake, fold in the nuts.

CREAM CHEESE ICING

1 (3 oz.) pkg. cream cheese,
softened
¼ cup light cream

2½ cups confectioners sugar
1 tsp. vanilla

Beat the cheese and the cream together vigorously with an electric mixer or by hand until they are smoothly blended.

Add in the sugar and the extract and beat again for about 2 minutes, or until the icing is fluffy.

CREAMY SMOOTH ICING

½ stick margarine or butter
2 cups confectioners sugar,
sifted

⅛ tsp. salt
1 tsp. vanilla
2 Tbsp. heavy cream

Cream the butter with 1½ cups of the sugar and the salt. Add in the remaining sugar alternately with the vanilla and the cream. Mix well until the icing is smooth and creamy.

Makes enough icing for two 8-inch layers or 2 dozen cupcakes.

EASY JELLY ICING

½ cup tart jelly
1 egg white, unbeaten

⅛ tsp. salt

Place the ingredients in a double boiler over boiling water and cook, beating constantly until the jelly is melted. Remove the pan from heat and continue beating until the mixture will hold its shape.

EGG YOLK ICING

3 egg yolks
½ cup granulated sugar

⅛ stick butter or margarine
Juice of one lemon

Cook the ingredients in a double boiler until they are thick. This is an economical and delicious icing.

FROZEN STRAWBERRY ICING

1 lb. confectioners sugar   ½ pkg. frozen strawberries,
1 stick margarine   thawed (drain slightly)

Beat the ingredients together and spread between the layers and on top of cake.

HONEY BUTTER ICING

2 sticks butter   4 egg whites, stiffly beaten
½ cup honey   2 squares unsweetened
2 cups confectioners sugar   chocolate, melted

Cream together the butter, the honey, and the sugar. Then gradually beat in the egg whites. Pour into this the melted chocolate. Blend well. Spread over the top and the sides of the cake and between the layers.

LEMON CREAM BUTTER ICING

2 cups sifted confectioners   Grated rind of one lemon
                          sugar   ½ stick butter, softened
2 Tbsp. lemon juice

Blend together the sugar, lemon juice and lemon rind. Add the softened butter and stir it in thoroughly. When the mixture is velvety smooth, spread it over the top and the sides of the cake.

MAPLE ICING

1 stick butter   6 Tbsp. milk
4 cups confectioners sugar,   1 tsp. maple flavoring
                          sifted

Cream the butter; add in the sugar gradually. Add the milk and the flavoring. Beat until the icing is smooth.

ONE MINUTE FUDGE ICING

2 Tbsp. cocoa

1 cup granulated sugar

½ stick butter

¼ tsp. salt

¼ cup light cream

¼ tsp. vanilla

1 Tbsp. white syrup

Cook the ingredients together over low heat for one minute; stir constantly. Then beat steadily until the icing is very smooth.

ORANGE ICING

¼ stick butter

1 (1 lb.) box confectioners
sugar

1 tsp. lemon extract

Juice, rind, and pulp of 1
orange

Blend the butter with the sugar. Stir in the lemon extract, the orange juice, rind and pulp. Stir steadily until the mixture is quite smooth.

PEANUT BUTTER ICING

2 cups light brown sugar

6 Tbsp. heavy cream

⅜ stick butter

1 Tbsp. peanut butter

1 cup confectioners sugar

½ tsp. vanilla

Stir the brown sugar, the cream and the butters together in a saucepan over low heat. As soon as the mixture starts to boil, remove the pan from the heat and stir in the powdered sugar. Beat until the mixture is thick and smooth. Then stir in the vanilla.

SCOTCH COFFEE ICING

½ stick butter

½ cup brown sugar

3 cups confectioners sugar

¼ cup very strong coffee

Cream the butter; add the brown sugar and continue creaming. Then add the powdered sugar alternately with the coffee. Beat until the icing is of a consistency for spreading.

Pile thickly on the top and the sides of the cake; make deep swirls with the bottom of a large silver spoon as a decoration.

SNOW PEAK ICING

¾ cup white corn syrup	Pinch of salt
2 egg whites	1 tsp. vanilla

Heat the syrup to the boiling point. Meanwhile beat the egg whites with a hand or electric beater until they are stiff but not dry. Add the salt. Then slowly pour the syrup over the beaten egg whites, while continuing to beat, until the icing is fluffy and will stand in peaks from the beater. Fold in the vanilla.

Ices top of two 8 or 9-inch layers.

TUTTI FRUTTI ICING

12 maraschino cherries, drained and chopped	½ cup chopped figs, moist
	½ cup pecans, chopped

Double the recipe for Snow White Frosting (p. 167).

Remove one-third of the finished icing and stir in the above ingredients. Spread this combination between the cake layers.

Spread the remaining plain icing on the top and sides of the cake.

UNCOOKED ICING

¼ stick butter, softened	4½ Tbsp. evaporated milk
3 cups confectioners sugar	1½ tsp. vanilla

Blend all the ingredients together by stirring slowly until the mixture holds its shape. Then beat until the icing is velvety smooth.

YUMMY PINK ICING

1½ cups granulated sugar	1 tsp. vanilla
¼ tsp. cream of tartar	1 tsp. almond extract
2 large or 3 small egg whites	Red food coloring
5 Tbsp. cold water	

Mix together the sugar, cream of tartar, the egg whites and the cold water in a double boiler. Place the pan over boiling water. Beat constantly for several minutes with a rotary beater until the mixture has thickened.

Remove the pan from the fire and add in the vanilla and the almond extract. Blend well. Tint the icing pale pink with 3 or 4 drops of the red food coloring, and spread the icing at once on the cooled cake.

ALMOND GLAZE (For Fruit or Coffee Cakes)

1 cup confectioners sugar   ⅛ tsp. almond extract
1 Tbsp. water

Blend the ingredients together in a small bowl.
Dribble over the cake before serving, allowing the glaze to run down the sides of the cake. Decorate with a few whole almonds.

CINNAMON PINEAPPLE TOPPING

½ stick butter or margarine,   ½ cup crushed pineapple,
          melted   well-drained
⅔ cup light brown sugar   ⅓ cup flaked coconut
      firmly packed   1 Tbsp. pineapple juice
                                          ¼ tsp. ground cinnamon

Combine all the ingredients thoroughly. Spread over the top of baked and cooled cake.

CRUMB TOPPING

½ cup brown sugar   1¼ tsp. cinnamon
2 Tbsp. all-purpose flour   ¼ stick butter, softened

Blend together the sugar, the flour and the cinnamon. Cut in the soft butter until the mixture is crumbly.

GLAZE (For Fruit or Loaf Cake)

2 Tbsp. brown sugar   2 Tbsp. water
1 Tbsp. corn syrup

Combine the ingredients in a saucepan and place over low heat. Bring to a boil and simmer for two minutes. Brush over cake.

GREEN TINTED COCONUT

1 tsp. milk or water
Few drops of green food
        coloring

1⅓ cups flaked coconut

Place the milk or water in a bowl. Add the coloring and mix well. Add the coconut and toss it with a fork until the coconut is thoroughly tinted.

Makes enough to cover top and sides of a medium sized cake. (Before applying the coconut with the palm of your hand to the sides of cake, place a paper collar around the cake to catch loose coconut.)

HONEY NUT TOPPING (For Coffee Cake)

½ stick butter
4 Tbsp. granulated sugar
4 Tbsp. all-purpose flour

4 Tbsp. honey
½ cup chopped nuts

Cream the butter with the sugar; mix well. Add in the flour and the honey and beat until mix is smooth. Stir in the nuts.

Spread on coffee cakes before baking.

LEMON MERINGUE TOPPING

⅓ cup granulated sugar
3 Tbsp. all-purpose flour
1 egg yolk
⅛ tsp. salt
½ cup water

2 Tbsp. lemon juice
1 Tbsp. grated lemon rind
1/16 stick butter (1 tsp.)
3 egg whites
1 Tbsp. granulated sugar

Blend the sugar and the flour. Add in the egg yolk, the salt, water, lemon juice, lemon rind, and the butter. Cook in a double boiler until the mixture is thick and creamy; stir constantly as it cooks. Remove the pan from the fire; beat the contents well and allow them to cool until they are lukewarm. Then spread this topping onto the baked cake.

Now make the meringue by beating the egg whites until they are stiff. Add in the 1 Tbsp. of sugar and beat again until the whites hold a peak. Put the meringue over the topping and brown it by placing the topped cake under the broiler for a few minutes. Serve the cake immediately.

STREUSEL TOPPING

¼ cup flour   4 tsp. cooking oil
½ cup granulated sugar

Mix the flour and the sugar in a small bowl. Gradually add the cooking oil; toss to distribute well.

LEMON SAUCE

1 Tbsp. cornstarch   ¾ cup water
¾ cup granulated sugar   ⅛ stick butter
1 egg, separated   2 Tbsp. lemon juice
¼ tsp. salt   ⅛ tsp. grated lemon rind

Mix the cornstarch, sugar, egg yolk, salt, and the water with a rotary beater. Place the mix in a double boiler and cook it for 5 minutes, stirring constantly. Remove the pan from the heat and add in the butter, the lemon juice, and the rind. Let the mixture cool.

Beat the egg white until it is frothy and fold it into the sauce.

LEMON RAISIN SAUCE

⅓ cup granulated sugar   ½ cup raisins
1 Tbsp. cornstarch   1 tsp. lemon juice
¼ tsp. cinnamon   ⅛ stick butter
1½ cups water

In a saucepan blend the sugar, cornstarch and cinnamon. Add in the water and cook over medium heat, stirring constantly until the mixture comes to a boil. Add in the raisins and simmer 2 to 3 minutes. Remove the pan from the heat and add in the lemon juice and butter. Stir until the butter is dissolved, then let the sauce cool before serving it.

Common Causes and Remedies in Cake ☙ Baking Failures

COMMON CAUSES AND REMEDIES IN CAKE
BAKING FAILURES

LAYER CAKES, POUND CAKES, and so forth.

A) DEFECT: Cakes Sink in Center

CAUSE	REMEDY
1. Insufficient moisture.	1. Increase liquid to proper absorption.
2. Inferior shortening.	2. Use special hydrogenated shortening for best results.
3. Improper mixing.	3. Follow accurately the mixing speed and time specified in recipe being used.
4. Improper oven temperature.	4. For best results, use oven temperature of 350°—never over 375°.
5. Inferior flour.	5. Use only high quality cake flour for best results.
6. Under-baking.	6. Do not disturb cakes until batter has "set," or until baked in center.

B) DEFECT: Cakes Expand, Then Fall during Baking

1. Too much moisture.	1. Due to climatic conditions, flour will sometimes pick up moisture in storage, thus altering the moisture content of the formula. If batter is already mixed, add more flour.
2. Inferior flour.	2. Use high quality cake flour.
3. Poor emulsification.	3. Use special hydrogenated cake shortening, or half shortening and half butter.
4. Too much baking powder.	4. Reduce amount.
5. Over-creaming.	5. Reduce speed and creaming time of shortening.
6. Too low oven temperature.	6. Regulate oven temperature before placing cakes in oven.

C) DEFECT: Cakes Shrink or Pull from Sides of Pan

1. Too much liquid.	1. Balance formula. If batter is already mixed, add more flour.

CAUSE	*REMEDY*
2. Poor emulsification.	2. Check quality of shortening. Use high grade hydrogenated shortening or half shortening and half butter.
3. Wrong temperature of ingredients when mixed.	3. All ingredients, especially the eggs, liquid and shortening should be between 70 and 80° when mixed.
4. Unbalanced formula.	4. Check, measure and weigh all ingredients, as the case may be, carefully. Do not use guess work in this very important step.
5. Over-baking.	5. Bake only enough to set the cake.
6. Not enough batter in pans.	6. Increase amount of batter.
7. Oven too cold or too hot.	7. Regulate oven at 350° before placing cakes in it.
8. Improper cooling.	8. Remove cakes from pans as soon as possible and cool on special cake racks, free from drafts.
9. Inferior flour.	9. Use high grade cake flour.
10. Mix too plain and "bready."	10. Increase proportion of eggs, sugar and shortening.
11. Over-mixing.	11. Cut down speed and time of mixing.
12. Too much leavening.	12. Reduce baking powder.

D) DEFECT: *Poor Volume*

1. Oven too hot.	1. Regulate oven at 350° while mixture is being prepared.
2. Insufficient leavening.	2. Increase amount of leavening agent.
3. Excess leavening.	3. Cut down amount of leavening agent.
4. Under-mixing.	4. Use speed and full time given in the recipe especially in last stage.
5. Mix too plain and "bready."	5. Increase amount of eggs and shortening.
6. Weak or watery eggs.	6. Be sure eggs are fresh, if using shell eggs.
7. Improper measuring.	7. Check weights of ingredients carefully.

CAUSE	REMEDY
8. Poor emulsification.	8. Check shortening. Use only special hydrogenated shortening.
9. Excess moisture.	9. Reduce amount of liquid.
10. Not sufficient moisture.	10. Increase amount of liquid.
11. Improper mixing temperature.	11. Batter should be 70 to 80° and not over 80°.

E) DEFECT: Coarse Grain

1. Over-mixing.	1. Check formula and use correct mixing speed and time.
2. Cold oven.	2. Regulate oven at 350°.
3. Too much leavening.	3. Reduce amount of leavening agent, especially at high altitudes.
4. Unbalanced formula.	4. Measure and weigh all ingredients carefully.
5. Insufficient moisture.	5. Increase liquid.
6. Under-mixing.	6. Give correct speed and full mixing time.
7. Too much sugar.	7. Reduce amount.
8. Poor shortening.	8. Use special hydrogenated shortening.
9. Too high speed on mixer.	9. Use slower speeds in early stages.
10. Too much shortening or egg yolk.	10. Reduce amounts accordingly.
11. Wrong type of flour.	11. Use high grade cake flour.
12. Batter stands too long before baking.	12. Batter should be baked as soon after mixing as possible.

F) DEFECT: White Cakes Off-Color

1. Off-color shortening.	1. Use best quality shortening.
2. Poor flour.	2. Use high quality cake flour.
3. Poor baking powder.	3. Use best grade.
4. Poor egg whites.	4. Check for quality and freshness.
5. Wrong mixing temperature.	5. Best mixing temperature is between 70 and 80°.
6. Not enough acidity.	6. Add cream of tartar or phosphate.
7. Insufficient mixing.	7. Increase speed and mixing time.

G) DEFECT: *White Cakes Bake Out Yellow*

CAUSE	REMEDY
1. Too much soda.	1. Cut down on soda or use a little cream of tartar or phosphate.
2. Excess invert sugar.	2. Cut down on amount.
3. Poor shortening.	3. Use special hydrogenated shortening.
4. Poor egg whites.	4. Check for freshness.
5. Poor cake flour.	5. Use high grade cake flour.

H) DEFECT: *Whole Egg Cakes Have Greenish Tint*

1. Too much soda.	1. Reduce amount.
2. Frozen eggs too old.	2. Use fresh frozen eggs as soon as thawed.
3. Mixing temperature too low.	3. Use temperature between 70 and 80°.

I) DEFECT: *Soggy Streaks in Cakes*

1. Excess moisture.	1. Cut down on liquid.
2. Excess leavening.	2. Use less baking powder.
3. Excess acid in mixture.	3. Cut down on sour milk, phosphate, cream of tartar, and so forth.
4. Insufficient mixture of dry ingredients.	4. Sift together all dry ingredients one or more times.
5. Excessive top oven heat.	5. Bake in uniform oven.
6. Poor flour.	6. Use high grade cake flour.
7. Improper cooling.	7. Do not ice cakes until cooled.
8. Cakes knocked in oven.	8. Handle cakes carefully during baking, do not jar.
9. Under-baked.	9. Bake until cakes are well set.

J) DEFECT: *Cakes Crack in Baking*

1. Batter too stiff.	1. Add more liquid.
2. Over-mixing.	2. Cut mixing speed and time.
3. Oven too hot.	3. Lower heat and regulate to 350°.
4. Uneven oven heat.	4. Regulate oven to uniform heat before baking.
5. Excessive acid or soda.	5. Cut down on amount.
6. Mixture too poor and "bready."	6. Use more shortening and sugar.

K) DEFECT: *Crust Too Thick*

1. Too much sugar.	1. Reduce amount.
2. Oven too hot.	2. Reduce temperature.

CAUSE	REMEDY
3. Too long in oven.	3. Bake shorter time at higher temperature.
4. Weak flour.	4. Use best grade cake flour.

L) DEFECT: Crust Peels and Flakes Off

1. Too much steam in oven.	1. Open oven damper slightly.
2. Oven too cool.	2. Raise temperature accordingly and regulate.
3. Weak eggs.	3. Check for freshness and quality.
4. Weak flour.	4. Use best grade cake flour.
5. Poor formula.	5. Check for proper balance.

M) DEFECT: Cakes Peak Up in Center or on Side

1. Mixture too lean.	1. Add more shortening and sugar.
2. Not enough leavening.	2. Add more baking powder.
3. Insufficient moisture.	3. Add more liquid.
4. Over-mixing.	4. Cut mixing speed and time.
5. Flour too hard.	5. Use best cake flour.
6. Too much flour.	6. Add more liquid.
7. Oven too hot.	7. Reduce temperature accordingly.

N) DEFECT: Cakes Are Tough

1. Poor flour.	1. Use high grade cake flour.
2. Over-mixing.	2. Cut down on speed and mixing time.
3. Over-baking.	3. Cut baking time.
4. Mixture too plain and "bready."	4. Increase shortening and sugar.
5. Excess egg whites.	5. Cut down on amount accordingly.
6. Oven too cool.	6. Raise temperature accordingly.
7. Eggs not beaten enough.	7. Beat eggs to proper volume, especially in sponge cakes.
8. Insufficient richness.	8. Add more shortening and sugar.

O) DEFECT: Cakes Too Tender to Handle

1. Excess sugar.	1. Reduce amount accordingly.
2. Excess shortening.	2. Reduce amount accordingly.
3. Excess leavening.	3. Reduce amount accordingly.
4. Under-mixing.	4. Increase mixing time.
5. Over-mixing.	5. Cut speed and mixing time.
6. Poor flour.	6. Use good grade cake flour.
7. Not enough eggs.	7. Increase amount accordingly.

P) DEFECT: Cakes Dry Out Too Rapidly

CAUSE	REMEDY
1. Climatic conditions.	1. Use invert sugar.
2. Insufficient shortening.	2. Increase amount accordingly.
3. Insufficient sugar.	3. Increase amount accordingly.
4. Poor shortening.	4. Use hydrogenated cake shortening.
5. Too few eggs.	5. Increase amount accordingly.
6. Too much leavening.	6. Reduce amount accordingly.
7. Oven too cool.	7. Raise temperature accordingly.
8. Over-baked.	8. Bake only until cakes are set.
9. Insufficient moisture.	9. Increase amount of liquid or egg accordingly.

Q) DEFECT: Cakes Mold Quickly

1. Bad storage.	1. Store in dry, well ventilated room.
2. Contamination.	2. Check storage room for sources of contamination.
3. Improper cooling.	3. Do not pack or store until cool.

R) DEFECT: Uneven Texture

1. Poor shortening.	1. Use hydrogenated cake shortening.
2. Under-mixing.	2. Follow mixing instructions in formula.
3. Over-mixing.	3. Use low speed in first stages of mixing.
4. Too much liquid.	4. Reduce amount accordingly.
5. Insufficient sugar.	5. Increase amount accordingly.
6. Wrong oven conditions.	6. Check for temperature, drafts, and so forth.
7. Mixing speed too high.	7. Use low speeds.
8. Mixing temperature too warm or too cold.	8. Mix between 70 and 80°.

S) DEFECT: Dark Spots on Bottom of Cakes

1. Undissolved sugar.	1. Use fine granulated sugar.

ANGEL FOOD AND SUNSHINE CAKES

A) DEFECT: Cakes Shrink from Sides and Bottom of Pans

1. Oven too hot.	1. Regulate oven to temperature stated in recipe.

CAUSE	REMEDY
2. Air pockets between cakes and pans.	2. Gently knock pans to work mixture down before placing in oven.
3. Flour too hard.	3. Use best quality cake flour.
4. Grease in pans.	4. Wash in hot water and rinse in cool water just before using.

B) DEFECT: Spots and Thick Crust on Top of Cakes

1. Baked too long.	1. Bake until set only.
2. Poor flour.	2. Use high grade cake flour.
3. Undissolved sugar.	3. Use fine granulated sugar.
4. Temperature too slow.	4. Increase temperature.

C) DEFECT: Cakes Fall When In or Out of Oven

1. Oven too hot.	1. Reduce temperature accordingly.
2. Egg whites whipped too much.	2. Reduce whipping time. Do not whip whites dry.
3. Egg whites whipped at wrong temperature.	3. Whip at temperature between 70 and 80°.
4. Pans contain too much moisture.	4. Turn pans upside down and drain off excess water just before using.
5. Too much liquid.	5. Do not add water to mixture.
6. Improperly cooled.	6. Invert cakes in pans on rack to cool.

D) DEFECT: Cakes Stick In Pans and Cannot Be Removed

1. Pans too dry.	1. Rinse pans in cool water and drain just before filling with mixture.
2. Soiled pans.	2. Keep pans and other utensils thoroughly clean.

E) DEFECT: Dark Cakes

1. Poor acidity.	1. Use pure cream of tartar.
2. Old or weak eggs.	2. Check eggs for freshness and quality.
3. Soiled mixing utensils.	3. Utensils must be thoroughly clean and free from grease.
4. Unbleached flour.	4. Use best quality cake flour.

Important. Careless measuring usually means failure. Failure, in turn, means waste. Waste means loss of money, time, and energy, and—worst of all—discouragement.

Index

INDEX